ASYMPTOTES AT THE INFINITY OF PASSION:

THE UNTOUCHABLE QUEST OF POETRY

JEAN-YVES SOLINGA

FIRST EDITION

Little Red Tree Publishing, LLC,
635 Ocean Avenue, New London, CT 06320

Previous works published with Little Red Tree Publishing:

Clair-Obscur of the Soul (2008)
Clair-obscur de l'âme [in French] (2008)
In the Shade of a Flower (2009)
Landscape of Envies (2010)
Words Made of Silk (2011)
Impressions of Reality (2013)
Artist in a Pixelated World (2014)

Copyright © 2015 Jean-Yves Solinga

All rights are reserved under International and Pan-American Copyright Conventions. Except for brief passages quoted in a newspaper, magazine, radio or television review, no part of this book may be reproduced in any form or by any means, electronic or mechanical, including photocopying and recording, or by any information storage and retrieval system, without permission in writing from the publisher.

Layout and Cover Design: Michael Linnard, MCSD
Text in Forum, Times New Roman, Trajan Pro and Ariel.

First Edition, 2015, manufactured in USA
1 2 3 4 5 6 7 8 9 10 LSI 20 19 18 17 16 15

Library of Congress Cataloging-in-Publication Data

Solinga, Jean-Yves
 Asymptotes at the Infinity of Passion: The Untouchable Quest of Poetry / Jean-Yves Solinga. -- 1st ed.
    p. cm.
  Includes glossary and index.
  ISBN 978-1-935656-39-5 (pbk. : alk. paper)
  I. Title.
  PS3612.A58565S77 2015
  811'.6--dc23

Little Red Tree Publishing LLC
635 Ocean Avenue,
New London Connecticut 06320
www.littleredtree.com

Contents

Foreword by Michael Linnard	vii
Introduction by Jean-Yves Solinga	xi
PROLOGUE Return from Paris: A Manifesto	xvii
I IN LIEU OF A PAINTING	1
White Absolution	2
Ultimate Sensations	5
Frozen Land	6
Luciana	7
Le train bleu	8
Random Morsels	9
As the lights on the Eiffel Tower start to sparkle	11
In Paris: Saxophone solo	13
Erased Moments	14
Asymptotes at the Infinity of Passion	15
A Certain Languor in her Eyes	17
Une certaine lassitude dans les yeux	19
Last Supper	21
The Perfume of the Gods	23
Emotion Recollected in Tranquility	24
From both sides of the canvas	25
In Lieu of a Painting	26
Inner Sanctum	29
Reflected Gaze	30
The Nobility of Frailty	31
Sanctuary	32
Tremors from the Universe	34
Tremors from the Universe II	36

II	**THE REPLACEABLE SOLDIER**	37

The replaceable soldier	38
A Voice from Company C 4th Platoon	42
A Successful Life	43
Rorschach Inkblot Test	44
Rising from the mud	45
A Beautiful Baby	46
Through a child's eyes	48
Through a child's eyes II	49
A higher wall and different color	50
A saintly father	51
Shrapnel of Love	52
Personal Conscience and Collective Absolution	53
Convergence	54
The Human Face of Destiny	55
Historical Monument 3rd Quarter of Twentieth Century	56
Multiple Realities	57
Of Gypsies Jews and Others	59
Sleepwalkers of World War One	60
The Train Engineer	61
We… We didn't do anything wrong	62
Between the Jehovah Witness and the S&M Prostitute	63

III	**ART AND REALITY**	65

Trailways idyll	66
Cyrano: a fable	67
A Place at the Table	68
A Post Modern Woman	69
Androgyny	70
Appetite and Disdain	73
Art and Reality	74
Silky Reality	75
Billie Holiday and Édith Piaf	76
Stone Dust	78
Acculturation: Sounds of Snapping Crust.	79
French Kiss	79
Madeleines	80
Constructive Criticism	81

Esthetics of Cruelty	82
Raw Talent	83
Free Lunch	85
In a More Perfect World	86
Jesus… Aspiring Rabbi and Capable Carpenter	87
Taste of the New World	88
Exchange Student	89
The Un-protocoled Internet	90
African Fable	91
… and injustice for the rest of them all	92
A Fatherly Figure	93
The Accidental American	94

IV   GIVING A FACE TO THE ABSURD   95

Truth in Fiction	96
You Might Not Like What You Find	99
Rusty Landscape	100
Giving a Face to the Absurd	101
Fall from Perfection	102
Beast of Burden	103
My Refrigerator and Me	104
Don't Worry They're In Charge	106
In the Tramway Tunnel	108
The Glance upon the Other	109
Only One Second	111
Self Awareness	112
The Angle of the Sun… The Song of the Cicadas	113
The Tree the Atheist and Nothingness	114
Vaporous Truths	115
Just a Man in a Turtle Neck	116
The Genesis Revisited	118
Unmentionables	120
Habitable Zone	121

Glossary and Notes	123
Index [Titles and First Lines]	131
About the Author	137

Foreword

Remarkably, I am yet again presented with the task of writing a foreword in response to another outstanding collection of poems from my friend Jean-Yves Solinga, a task I take great pride in performing. In this book, *Asymptotes at the Infinity of Passion*, his eighth book of poetry, in as many years, Jean-Yves returns to grapple with his and Camus' definition of the core responsibility of the artist—poet in Jean-Yves' case—which is to distill ineffability and offer it in as aesthetic form as possible, so that we may access a fresh, revitalized vision of humanity and the world in which we all exist: From the small, intimate and personal private moments, to the big, public, international events that change the course of history. Essentially there is no subject matter that is too small or insignificant that can evade the attention of Jean-Yves.

Unfamiliar, as I and no doubt many of you are, with the word asymptote, I was pleasantly surprised to learn that I had been living with it most of my life. In fact, as a former professional furniture/interior designer and teacher of design, I have spent a life time working with the graphical implications and aesthetic qualities of the "dynamic curve" ...or in other words asymptotic constructions, with its asymmetry and geometric certainty of incompletion. It is the prefect analogy/metaphor to explain the process by which artists, since the dawn of existence, have sought to understand and explain the human condition: In other words, whilst accepting the infinite certainty of separation from absolute comprehension and description, a true artist relentlessly pursues understanding through their art form.

Jean-Yves endlessly explores humanity's perception of reality within an existentialist view of the absurdity of breathtaking beauty and unspeakable horror as they inhabit the same space and time. In his inimitable style of multilayered, multifaceted images his poems bring us both nearer to uncomfortable truths in which most would not willingly venture, or to a point of passion or beauty we could not have previously envisioned.

In previous books—you will find a full list after the title page—Jean-Yves has taken the time to describe over 30 pages or more of situations and scenarios that motivate or direct his muse. Suffice to say there appears no sign of these having been sated or become redundant in any way. In fact I believe that he expands and adds to them almost everyday.

While most writers wait for the muse to appear or reveal itself to them, to Jean-Yves every memory, event or visual stimulation has significance and potential, requiring an immediate response. Nothing in his conscious or, in fact, unconscious mind has irrelevance in the process of creating his poetry. Therefore, he writes constantly because for him, there is so much to write about. The human experience is indeed manifestly rich with endless possibilities.

I take just one example to illustrate my point. A teary smile of a grandmother, who sees resemblances of her son walk past her on the street might be an unimportant detail on its own or somewhat overly sentimental but Jean-Yves sets it against the giggles of teenage girls at his appearance, rendering both distinct yet immutable bound together. This juxtaposition of human responses and interactions is in the end what matters.

I encourage all those who are interested in poetry, that reaches out to explain the human experience at its extremes, to read this collection, it will enrich your soul as it did mine.

Michael Linnard
New London, CT. 2015

Acknowledgement

Little Red Tree Publishing and Michael Linnard have been at the inception of my poetry publication and in the process have been an integral part of my work. I am proud to say that, *Asymptotes at the Infinity of Passion*, is the eighth book in the collection of this steadfast support. I am particularly proud of Michael's relevantly beautiful cover, which brings into focus the city of Paris and the asymptotic curves of the Eiffel Tower.

With time, the writing and publishing of another book feels akin to a time capsule, a message in a bottle thrown in the water. Furthermore, it also has, especially in the first section, the appearance and tonality of very intimate and personal reflections written for what is after all: the public square.

In essence, for me, a book of poetry is, before all, a statement of concepts of my esthetics and ethics and it is with whatever value it contributes to a civilized culture that I proudly offer it in the name of persons who have made me who I am.

With a complement of presences, images, moments, memories and friends safe in my soul, it makes drinking a morning coffee or sitting at a good table in the middle of a New England winter feel like a fortress worthy of the one in my African youth.

But it is in the glorious vision of the future offered to me through my wife Elaine, my son Robert, his wife Elizabeth and their son Luc, my daughter Nicole Solinga-Stasi and her husband Marc and their daughters Noëlle and Luciana that I can humbly recognize and appreciate my emotional wealth.

Jean-Yves Vincent Solinga
Gales Ferry, Connecticut 2015

Introduction

I find the analogy of an asymptote a good visual for what a poet regularly resorts to in an attempt to *touch* an idea or an ideal: May that goal be political (injustice, prejudice), intimate (walking along the Seine when the lights on it start to sparkle), historic, societal (pollution, anti-Semitism, the indescribable horrors of war and the longing for peace) or cosmic (the future of mankind). None of these topics are by their nature and scope easily contained; but the natural density of poetry is well suited in reaching an approximate verbal description to mold the subject and try to apprehend it.

Albert Camus used the mythological Sisyphus pushing a rock endlessly up a hill to encapsulate the idea of the Absurd. It worked like a charm on my high school mind and sent me on a quest to know more about the Greek King and the French philosopher and to learn from both. And so, along the same visual equivalent, I have chosen the title *Asymptotes at the Infinity of Passion: the Untouchable Quest of Poetry* for this collection of poems.

An asymptote, generally speaking, is a line [value, point or limit] on a graph that is approached by another line [or value] but is *never touched*: This separation (no matter how minute) is kept into infinity.

I have often thought of the application of this concept when studying French Medieval poems. In some, the poet would look upon the figure of the Virgin Mary in her duality. That is: as a woman and a divinity. Both represented the unapproachable or untouchable presences: no matter the passion or intensity of the suitor or humble servant.

Thus, not withstanding the fervor or skill of the poet for the object of desire, the moment in the past, the reparation of injustice, the unspeakable horrors of such a thing as the enslavement of another, the product of the mind of the artist in front of such a challenge is going to feel wanting for something: compounded by the inapproachable and inenarrable make up of the topics.

It is along with the unbounded, unbridled, infinite passion of the poet's soul, that poetry tries to recreate and especially allow his reader to experience that same passion, that same moment, that same angst or that same anger through his art ["From Both Sides of the Canvas," "Esthetics of

Cruelty," "Reflected Gaze"]. It is telling that some poems make reference to the vision and intensity of artists such as Caravaggio, Courbet, and Renoir.

The sources of my poems in this work are what poems, at their best, must often be: the distilled ingredients of life and living. Tasting, reflecting and reviewing *moments*.

But by nature, and as a conscious esthetic choice, I like to avoid direct biographical references. Therefore in the rare or unavoidable occasions to the contrary, I willingly acknowledge the personal reference and if necessary give any helpful witnessed hints to reinforce and allow immediacy to the words ["Trailways Idyll," "Le train bleu"]. Although, at all time, with poetic license acting as a veil of protective fiction. And like Montaigne, looking for a universal trait locked in the particular act.

Therefore, rather than my particular life, I like to think that the reader would be more interested in the experiences of a Jorge Semprùn or a Primo Levi's: "Of Gypsies, Jews and Others," "Between the Jehovah Witness and the S&M Prostitute," "Historical Monument 3rd quarter of the Twentieth Century."

Nevertheless, even at its seemingly most intimate or personal, my lyrical poetry aims at a wider meaningful literary distance that a dab of fiction affords. I always look for the effect that form and substance take on from an outsider's viewpoint. So, even at its most voyeuristic, I treat my poetry as a movie script: Therefore... *the effect*. ["Return to Paris," "Sanctuary," "The Replaceable Soldier"]

In a quote of Zachary Leader by Sam Tarenhaus regarding Saul Bellow [n.y.t.b.r.]: "Bellow borrows real-life qualities and oppositions in drawing his characters, then exaggerates them to meet dramatic or fictional ends," Tarenhaus adds, "In other words, he [Bellow] was a *novelist*." [My italics]. I like that. It is for this reason that I never forget that I am writing poetry and not a biographical non-fiction. [I cannot get my head around the concept of bio-fiction, which sounds too much like non-alcoholic wine]

Some poems are purely personal or familial-folkloric experiences ["Luciana"], the historical critique or commentary ["The Train Engineer" and coexisting in the guilty contagion of the German occupation of France]. While others are *cosmic* ["Just a man in a turtle neck," "The Genesis Revisited." Others, historic or about social reflections about racial and gender issues ["A Place at the Table," "A Post Modern Woman," "Billie Holiday and Édith Piaf," "Androgyny."]

There are many tangential references to the general literary, philosophical and artistic schools of thoughts: Existentialism; Absurdism; Impressionism; Romanticism etc. It is not only my vision of what good, intelligent writing should use; but it is also a perfect short cut for making a point and or linking my poetry to a long and fertile line of human thought. As the adage goes: even atheistic writers make use of God or the Bible for artistic ends. ["Fall from Perfection," "Jesus… aspiring rabbi and capable carpenter."]

Paris ["As the lights on the Eiffel Tower start to sparkle"] plays (as usual) a privileged part in this book. The city, once more, took a life of its own as I began writing. It seems the French expression "les mots appellent les mots" [words bring out more words] is still in play here. A couple of poems set in the proverbial walk-up of some Parisian hotel room, in the ferment of the nineteen sixties and seventies ["In Lieu of a Painting," "Paris Saxophone Solo"], turned into more poems and especially into this verbal explosion of images that I decided to keep separately: "Manifesto" ["Return from Paris"]. It is a sort of blueprint/rite of passage catchall poem, containing all sorts of grievances, hopes and beliefs: the Vietnam War, Racism and the glory… the absolute un-reconstructability of youth… well… it may in the final analysis be possible to reconstruct the latter: using *infinite passion* as the paintbrush ["Tremors of the Universe"].

This collection of poems is divided into four sections that generally fall into reflections on my arbitrary determination of the various drives of mankind: its emotional side; its aggressive history; the societal side; and its place in the cosmos. I claim some author's privilege in the resulting insertion of particular poems: especially in the societal section. Furthermore, I chose a center default as well as a liberal capitalization policy at the beginning of the next verse.

Jean-Yves Vincent Solinga
Gales Ferry, CT. 2015

"And often, he who had chosen the fate of the artist because he felt himself to be different, soon realized that he can maintain neither his art nor his difference unless he admits that he is like the others."

"Et celui qui, souvent, a choisi son destin d'artiste parce qu'il se sentait différent, apprend bien vite qu'il ne nourrira son art, et sa différence, qu'en avouant sa ressemblance avec tous."

"The artist forges himself to the others, midway between the beauty he cannot do without and the community he cannot tear himself away from."

"L'artiste se forge dans cet aller retour perpétuel de lui aux autres, à mi-chemin de la beauté dont il ne peut se passer et de la communauté à laquelle il ne peut s'arracher."

Albert Camus, from Nobel Prize for Literature acceptance speech 1957

Prologue

Return from Paris: A Manifesto

City of lights seen through the prism of multiple realities

Parisian time is set at midnight:
When time takes the shape of a Salvador Dali hourglass.

Gloriously incestuous overlapping of angry street demonstrations
With the gentle shadings of a rite of passage carnival.

Natural odd sweetness of three bises on the cheeks,
Regardless of the combination of genders:
Only a university photo Idi needed to partake.

Shy recalcitrant ambassador of Napalm bombings and nuclear power:
Symbolically standing out of the summer rain
Under the main entrance protection of the portico of the Sorbonne.

Continuing antithesis in this academic neighborhood of
An obscure medieval theologian
In a land of strict republican secularism and
Apparently rampant hedonism.

Centuries giving the French a jaded political ease toward issues
Transformed into destructive puritanical interest elsewhere.

Purity of the natural sensuality of the senses
Exemplified in the simplest things and moments

Such as the acrid sweetness of a kingly Camembert
The complicated herbal taste of a Noilly Prat

The echoes of Renoir and a late summer afternoon
full of flowers in a woman's perfume

Ambivalent movie stars pouts, like Jeanne Moreau,
That say both... disdain and desire.

Feminine sexuality that hides its ambivalent leanings
Under close trimmed hair cut and chain-smoking aggression.

Accompanied by un-blinking eyelids allowing a glance
Into a dark soul full of burning embers akin to Manet's *Olympia*.

Swirling visions of pre-commitments.
Pre-career carefree days. Uncharted emotional landscape.

A place of intellectualized sidewalk café sensuality and sexuality.
No need for the bedroom-bound paper pulp fiction of Henry Miller
or art cinemas of "Last Tango in Paris":

These things can reveal themselves quietly, naturally in this city:
They can strike from above like to a young Lépold Senghor
Discovering the attraction of Africa's alternate happiness
In this city's reflections in the jungle-blackness of the Seine.

Uncanny wisdom from the concierge in binary English
Coming from an incorrigibly existentialist soul
Linked to the gravitas of a Camus and intonations
of an Inspector Clouseau.

"The setting incites it" he says.
"The cobble streets demand it."
"Don't forget revolutionary blood... Real blood has been spilled here."
"A blood of reality far from the safety of the
academic world of your history texts."

Christians martyred, Huguenots thrown from towers
Both in the name of the same God.
Bones neatly stacked in catacombs, now, under sex-shops,
Blissfully unaware of the continuum they represent.
In true Gallic tragedy, husbands as they were

taken away to the guillotine,
Seeing both their wives and mistresses for the last time
from these very widows.

Amidst all this…
A disarmingly simple introduction:

"Ah! C'est vous l'Américain!?"
While on the Colonnes Morris of la Place Blanche is advertised the
epitome of sixties mores cinema:
"Je t'aime."
"Moi… Non plus."

Double identity. Double meaning.
Contradictory meanings for a young man looking for the key…

City of consecrated hills to pagan and biblical gods
Montmartre at the top
All dressed in virginal limestone.

With Pigalle unapologetic hedonistic at its feet.

L'île de la Cité. Notre Dame de Paris.
Still haunted by the duality of Esmeralda:
Frollo's greened-eyed reminder of the formidable power
and weakness of his own flesh.

Which passport should I use? They laugh at Americans seeing
communists everywhere.
God damn war!

All I want is a cheap couscous. And un vin gris.
And her glance. That glance!
How can so much be said without a sound!

All of these thoughts and images going through my head:
I can live for ten Francs a day!
Ah! To feel like a bohemian artist:
Like those hanging in the Musée d'Orsay.
Heartbreaking poetry and simple, pure heartbreaks.

Asymptotes at the Infinity of Passion

Verlaine and Rimbaud.
Rimbaud pretty like Jim Morrison.
Ah! Speak to me again my friend from Père Lachaise.

If you let yourself go, you can replenish your soul with Big Bang echoes
of tremors of the pages of history:

Such as le Jeu de Paume amplifying unalienable truths
within its neo-classical arches.
Victor Hugo could have had his daily mundane walk through this alley
And then, imagine Jean Valjean escaping to his destiny
through the sewers, from here.

Glorious overlap of multiple realities.
Feeling intoxicated by the intimate sounds from the flimsy hotel walls.
The magic of things invading the intimacy
of the most intimate corners of our lives

So that a humble bed is permitted to honor
the sinuous ocean-curves of an Odalisque
As they push into the willing softness of the mattress.

While down in the narrow streets,
New generations of lovers and dreamers
Wait their turn at the Movable Feast

Magical streets where one seems to viscerally acquire
a cultural complexity
From the black stains of centuries on the coarse granite-skin
of the monuments.

Religious icons of the past live in republican harmony
In the atheistic hearts of university students
The pagan soul of the city speaks instinctively through
unverbalized architectural truths.

Some places on Earth somehow can dispense with the
artifice of religious tablets
that speak of restrictive Canons of restraining guidance and
so-called ethical wisdom.

Prologue

Rather than the exhilarating fresh air of the
philosophy of the bedroom.

This… then, is what I have learned:

All that I had ever needed was to walk these streets.
Letting myself be possessed by the splendidly
non-aggressive androgyny permeating my pores.

An amoral peace whitewashing my years of acquisition
From the dusty archives of my studies.

Having, found out on this pivotal trip, in this pivotal place,
That it was not the learning that would untie me.

It was the letting go. Knowingly letting go.
Knowing WHAT it is that you are letting go.

What it is that you are giving back to the universe:
That part of you… deemed so precious.

So that, like Job, you can appear in front of your
last morsels of consciousness
Completely…Gloriously… NAKED.

When I return to the coldness of New England… the Labrador,
I will use this duality… these multiple realities.

I had been surrounded by apparently different identities and meanings
and yet, in the end, we all wanted the same things.

The duality of allegiance blurs lines incestuously.
I had felt only a distant kinship toward these places seen only on World
War Two fading photographs:
These people in the market of rue Saint Denis

Rushing to buy fresh leeks for Vichyssoise and summer tomatoes
for poulet à la Marengo
Would have been the very lives in my textbooks.

Paris-New York; The plane is ready to move.
Why is this seat empty?

They de-pressurize the cabin: my ears are plugged.
Why let this passenger in so late?
Well, at least she looks good in jeans.

"You almost missed the flight".
"Yes, my plane from Hanoi was late."

"Whoa! Americans can't travel there!"

[She reads English and French... No... It can't be her!]
"Your first name wouldn't be Jane by any chance?"
"Yes it is."

"Talking about Roger Vadim: Do you know how to cook?"

[Without skipping a beat and a disarming smile]
"You can't be married long to a Frenchman
without knowing how to cook."
[In my heart: It made up for Barberella]

"What do you do? I'm a French teacher".
"Oh!... In a little town. You wouldn't know it."

America love it or leave it. Vietnam or Montréal.
"Trying to be the best immigrant I can be."
All of these questions waiting for me back in this troubled New World.

"Why don't you come see me in New Haven."
"I'll be talking at a Black Panthers rally."

"The FBI will be waiting for us at the gate in New York."

"Damn! I had to declare that I was not a communist sympathizer
When I applied for my teaching job."

Good old days of clearly delineated bogeymen
on both sides of the issues.

Gun-ho capitalists and Che Guevara idealists

"I checked off the box that I would not incite the overthrow
Of the U.S. government and its institutions."

[For God sake! What I am doing next to her!]
[My mother had told me that our letters from France had been read
and then resealed. They could be already after me]

Still daydreaming at 30,000 feet

[I need this job.]
Damn! What would I have said?
"Are you telling us that your seating next to this person was by chance?"

Basic foundations of good citizenship.
"Yes. I do believe in democracy"

Half-asleep over the Atlantic:

[Now riding on a bus from Petersburg Virginia to D.C]

"No I don't understand why she cannot sit with me
because she's black."

"No I don't understand how this Vietcong threatens my freedom."

"Do you think Edgar Hoover heard what we said to each other?
Apparently he taped everybody else."

"You mean the argument is that Martin Luther King's ideas
were wrong or bad because he could not turn down easy sex?"

You should go to Paris!
Hear what they say about how dangerously up-tight Americans are.

It makes you wonder how the Washington media
would have handled Mary Magdalene.

A whore among all these men!
How can you listen to this guy?

Was The Christ really alone in Gethsemane?
Or was she with him in the dark?

Great men before their great day.
And we have all these little men:

Effeminates, like Edgar Hoover, sublimating
through listening in at keyholes.

Presidential ambitions retarding the Paris talks
Giving time to type more draft notices to soak maternal eyes.

I'm safe now at 30,000 feet
Elbow to elbow with the woman who would become
The voice of the rice farmers looking inquisitively
at Skyhawk bombers.

She belonged to the brotherhood and sisterhood
of those who would indeed help the enemy
And wait decades to wear their shroud of human decency.

She would be the unbeknownst spiritual sister
Of Mai Van On,
In the watery Vietnamese mud
Who dared help the "enemy" pilot on his own fateful day.

Do you think they'll arrest you in New York?

The F.B.I. agent [buzz haircut and insurance salesman suit]
looking at me and my yellow snickers:

"Miss Fonda… are you alone…?"
"Yes I am."

A few weeks later in front of my French class:

"Bonjour classe! I just came back from Paris"

"Bonjour Monsieur: Did anything interesting happen on your trip?"

Prologue

Poem provoked by a rush of images, thoughts and second thoughts about events in the author's past prompted by Democracy in the Dark: The Seduction of Government Secrecy *by Frederick A.O. Schwartz, JR, the repulsive and hypocritical abuses of J.Edgar Hoover and his hatred of Marin Luther King, the unexplainable sacrifices demanded for an opaque Viet Nam war and seeming breath of moral fresh air in the mores of sixties and early seventies in France.*

Paris... on the way to end of year lunch 2014.

I

IN LIEU OF A PAINTING

White Absolution

Lifted…
The coarse blanket of worldly problems,
With its streaks of gray organic filth from societal angst.

Dogmatic and petrified ideologies,
Rampant hypocrisy,
Insufferable suffering in the name of the sufferers.

Gigantic issues of runaway capitalism and modern-day servitude:
Building and destroying… over and over again.

Solace in this cocoon of antimatter… Of benign freezing whiteness.
White absolution…
Pregnant with hedonistic and amoral beauty.

Permeating lyricism truly possessing him viscerally,
In the mannerism of the other prophets of humanity.

The landscape in this apparently mundane world
unreservedly… gloriously, displaying the nobility of nothingness,

With the simplicity of a blank irreligious tablet…
A slate of innocence… of what counts:
A splendid and dignified display of the unwavering grandeur of just a
man… made it possible.

A plot and dénouement,
With no more importance than the next glance into
the intimate eyes of tomorrows.

This in a frozen land where frozen minuscule moments
Could do what armies and religions,
Philosophers and liars could not,

Transform—without the artifice of rituals—the very human
And still moist flesh next to him,

Into the eternal symbol of divine transmutation:
So dear to societies and yet so natural to lovers.

A representation of Doctor Zhivago and Larissa looking at the Siberian whiteness

Another lunch: a traditional "pot-au-feu" with hearty Moulin à vent wine. Saint Germain-des-Prés. Winter 2014.

Ultimate Sensations

"To live and die in Paris"* (revisited)

A gentleness in his consciousness of life:
As if being swaddled by things.

To be possessed… If not by love,
And if not by reality,

Then by their appearance:

Such that, for moments to exist,
Did not need their reincarnations in his embrace.

And so, when he felt life leaving him…

The tears, created by this immemorial rite of passage
—That we call dying—

Were misinterpreted as signs of pain
By the Parisian emergency services.

When in his reality,
They were still the result of his pure and continuing surprise
Of the ecstasy of the senses.

**"To Live and Die in Paris" from* Clair-Obscur of the Soul (2008).

Frozen Land

Outside ice and snow:
seemingly enraged by the lyrical arrogance of burning lyricism.

Torrid settings displayed in lacy poetry.
Beads of sweat seen as lithium flashes on wrinkled bed.

Exhausted breathless sighs gleefully competing with howling winds.
Dis-incarnated embraces solidly recreating past happiness.

Oblivious to the realities that are part of time,
are sharp edged pieces that could have made up the next hour
full of impending loneliness and a recurring cycle of routine.

Instead…
the reader is regaled with images of pregnant
emotional chaos and wild-eyed indulgences

That free the soul well before the body,
in an amoral pagan convergence of need and disponibility:

a state of mind exists that refuses to know the cold wind
of February and the frost on the trees.

Through pure fervor the sterile whiteness has become a canvas,
set up in the middle of a reconstructed landscape
of undulating palm trees and unhindered hedonism.

A frozen land of a gentle genesis
marrying bare flesh and flowing breezes:

In order to recover lost paradisiacal instants,
in a welcoming temple to immemorial souvenirs,
strewn with warm sheets and cooled by long eyelashes.

Antidote to a New England cold: writing poetry in a blizzard à la Doctor Zhivago

Luciana

Symbolic translucence of pinkish softness.
Surprising hints of tomorrows,
wrapped in the fragility of youthful genesis.

―――――――――――――――――――――――

Peaceful satisfied somnolence
found in the innocence of her soul.

When a transfixed and transfixing glance,
made of flashes of her luminescence,

somehow felt like an eternal drink of my fervent wishes,
while in return rained upon me drops of immortal hope.

A chance reciprocal look into the eyes of my grand-daughter Luciana (b. July 25, 2014)

Le Train Bleu*

It is not enough to have means.
Not enough to have life.

It is to deny to the end the definition of death.

That is… to throw into the void that waits
elements… no matter how insignificant,

elements…
of what nothingness is not.

It was in the Oh! … so natural movement of his hand!
The reciprocal mirror-image of hers,

and the resulting crystalline clinking of the Limoges glasses.

All of it… to the secret musical accompaniment in the memories
contained in their souls
and of a knowing hint of a smile on wrinkled lips,

that all had been said and all had been done by these two beings:
to honor living over death.

Witnessing a strikingly elegant older couple eating slowly, heartily and deliberately a stupendous lunch at le Train Bleu.

* Famous restaurant at the gare de Lyon in Paris [Renowned not only for the quality of its food but also the start of the iconic Orient Express]

To the music of "Paris Deluxe Chill Out Lounge Café HD"

Random Morsels

In homage to dying with a smile... with just a simple tear.

The purity... The unfiltered nature of it.

The natural... The human occurrence,
of what it is to slip into moments,
into instants of unguided hedonism,

running majestically... innocently nude...
through pieces of the universe:
finding the future in everyone and everything.

Biting into random morsels,
and rediscovering the dis-incarnated taste
of what it was to believe, for an infinitesimal eternity,

In a hint... in the vaguest of hope,
of happiness existing.

To be of the fraternity of the Happy Few:
of those of have learned... who KNOW...

how to make sparkle the last ember of consciousness.

To the music of the first cut of "The TAO Lounge 2."

Eiffel Tower in the moon light.

As the Lights on the Eiffel Tower Start to Sparkle…

To the flowers of Paradise

The virility of the musical pulse:
Repetitive bass countered by ethereal notes.

From the visceral center of digitized artificial waves:
Conceivable only in the recesses of human dreams.

Veuve Clicquot rosé on his lips,
Mixing with the saltiness of her moisture.

Anticipated pounding against his chest,
Coming from all directions.

Magical mixture of the next few seconds:
Anticipation of her pearls of fertilized happiness
submissively received,

As they honor what can only count for us mortals:
The jealous envy of the gods.

"Paris is for Lovers (My Love)" written by Tomas Høffding, from the album "Hotel Amour" by the group Terranova.

Les quais de la Seine, across l'île de la Cité and Notre Dame de Paris. (2014)

In Paris: Saxophone Solo*

Homage to Léopold Senghor "À New York (pour un orchestre de jazz: solo de trompette)"

Musical phrase coming up…

Magical alchemic intersection where dead black dots, on dead cellulose,
Turn into incarnations of sweat and receptive glances.

Subterranean Big Bang-vibrations of bass guitar,
Halting tease of the skin of the bass-drum,

Choreographed rhythms of glorious intimacy,
Solidity of the transmutation of the whispers of eye lashes
Closing on the threshold of exhausted happiness.

―――――――――――

Sensuality of fingers on critical glistening keys…
a quick unconscious breath,
A gentle nibble on the properly pre-moistened reed,
Mouth piece barely touching the lips,

Imperceptible warm flow creating echoes
Made of the surprising malleability of metallic sighs:
As offerings from the carnal depths of eternal moments…

Thus releasing into the nuptial cocoon
in this part of the privileged universe,
Undulating wavelets of the tremors of ecstasy.

*To the sound of "TAO Lounge 11"

Erased Moments

To the invisible lovers of history

There are those who have loved.
There are those who have stood in the limelight,
And thus, could dare think more of their hurt.

Unlike the smaller people...
Those nevertheless with big sighs:
The Wonder Bread kind.

Little people not seen or heard:
Not since that first meeting... Glances and words:
Who came and passed into those Wonder Bread nights.

Their aches, achievements and strengths evaporated.
Their names...
Mere steamy vapors in anonymous proletariat nights:
Those not found on the permanency of onion-skin biblical ones.

And yet their songs... Still worthy of the complexity of rarefied chords.
Their intimacy still suited for their earned share of ideals:
The ones more often reserved for the Classical genesis of the truly greats.

Their love,
Not diminished by the forgotten footnote that it has become.

And though... No temple columns had to be taken down,
No armies defeated,

We have in this Wonder Bread night... Simply two, who have loved,
And who are now hauntingly and plaintively resurrected.

Inspired by Regina Spektor's "Samson."

Asymptotes at the Infinity of Passion

Man of ardent fervor ... an artist.

Grasping…
Wanting to apprehend what he sees,
What he saw… What touched him.

Wanting to unrepentantly feel again what he had felt:
Preparing, in solidarity, a similar moment for Others.

Verbalizing, with his art,
A perfumed infinity of lyricism.

Creativity…
Acting as an antidote for the harsh reality of Time
That lives on his side of his art.

Privileged state… That of half-sleep.

Fertile landscape, where illusions can, at their will,
Invade the mind with delusional concepts of the
immortality of happiness.

Leaving streaks of the sweetness of sorrows on his pillow:
Children from the ferment of human memory.

By now, the artist fully awake,
Apprehensively faces the blank perspective of the white canvas;
The still inert keys of the piano;
The tear of black ink on the quill ready to destroy itself on the page.

He is now left with, as his only tool,
The infinity of his passion,

Unchanged since a hirsute caveman, with still vivid images in his eyes.
Walked to the smoky back corner of the grotto.

Or a heartbroken artist wanted to capture the double pain
of his infidelity multiplied by hers.

The whole experience, as part of the agonizing
immediacy and inapproachability
Of ephemeral sparkles of truth, beauty and happiness:

That define, by their very fragility,
What human conscience is.

An asymptote is a straight line approached, but never touched, by a given curve as one of the variables in the equation approaches infinity. [see introduction]

A Certain Languor in her Eyes

A certain languor in her eyes,
Across from his… of flames and inquisition.

She reacted with a gesture… with a hint of capitulation…
Of weakening,
Foretold through her futile interest in the activity of the bistrot.

A veil of tenderness enveloping the tone of her voice,
As though to help guide his fall.

A modesty in her posture… a majestic restraint,
The nobility of a richly layered personality
Which had so often given her a surprisingly gentle dominating ease upon
her intimates.

She seemed now resigned for a stalemate:
Between presences claiming her soul, her body,
but especially… her heart.

Suspecting another object of her affection,
He had tried to determine its nature:

Aware of her ambivalent taste…
Exasperated by his never having been chosen as the object of her
unguarded unconditional passion,

He thus had settled to remain in the cottony softness of fiction
Rather than impale himself on nails of reality:
Happiness made precious by the fragility of the film separating it from
this very reality

Incapable of denying him his share of lubricity,
She existentially needed to differentiate the limits of his claims on her.

He thus had avoided direct glances under the luxurious folds of her soul
Where could be detected someone else's image:

Not unlike these aisles leading to the Holy of Holies
Up to the feet of icons of some deities:
Those that deign ignore direct questions from us… Mere mortals.

His life at her side had become an allegorical world
Where reality would be sketches on the walls of her soul:

A mythical grotto
Where an intimate space had been reserved for a vaporous vestal shape
Of which he could only recognize a shapely silhouette
As wetness on the rock.

Fearful that enforced truth
Would leave him with aftertastes of blasphemes
Towards his muse,

He was falling prey to the polluted springs
Of vague hints, anguish, misery…
And a very earthly… distastefully mundane… jealousy.

Reading the presence of another in the eyes of the woman he loves: Inspired by "La fille aux yeux d'or" by Honoré de Balzac

Une certaine lassitude dans les yeux

Une certaine lassitude dans ses yeux:
Face aux siens brillants d'inquisition.

Elle fit un geste indiquant un soupçon de capitulation…
D'affaiblissement :
Dévoilé par son intérêt futile envers l'activité du bistrot.

Un voile de douceur enveloppait le ton de sa voix,
Comme pour adoucir sa chute.

Maintien de pudeur. Une retenue.
Les émanations majestueusement élégantes de son âme
Lui avait toujours offert une douce domination sur ses proches.

Elle semblait avoir pourtant déclaré une sorte de match nul
Entre les présences qui revendiquaient
Son âme, son corps, mais surtout… son cœur.

Ayant ressenti un autre objet de son affection,
Il avait essayé d'en déterminer la nature.

Il était conscient de la richesse et ambivalence de ses goûts :
Mais sans jamais en connaître la vraie passion.

Il s'était donc résigné de rester dans la douceur de la fiction
Au lieu de souffrir les clous de la réalité :

Convaincu que ce qui rend le bonheur si précieux
Est la fragilité du film qui le sépare de cette réalité.

Ne pouvant lui nier sa part de lubricité
Elle ne voulait pas qu'il confonde la limite de la sienne
À celles qu'elle avait attitrées aux autres.

Cela lui évita un regard direct entre les plis de son âme
Où il se devinait l'image d'une autre.

Comme ces déambulatoires vers les Saints des Saints
Montant aux pieds de certains dieux
Qui refusent l'interrogation directe des pauvres mortels.

Sa vie avec elle était devenue un monde allégorique
Où une surréalité se dessinait sur l'âme de cette femme,

Une grotte mythique :
Où un espace intime avait été réservé à une forme vestale
Dont il ne pouvait distinguer que la silhouette sinueuse
Sous forme suintante sur la pierre.

Il n'insista jamais à tout savoir, ayant peur des après goûts de blasphèmes
envers cette muse adorée :

Ne voulant pas faire preuve de jalousie trop humaine.

Lisant la présence d'une autre dans les yeux de la femme qu'il aime,
Inspiré de « La Fille aux yeux d'or d'Honoré de Balzac ».

Last Supper

Torture of the energy of images and sounds.
Discordance of incestuous voice tracks.

Film… mutually in slow motion and fast forward:
Living the experience of time travel.

But without the poets' artifice of opiates:
Just the immemorial passion of heartbreak.

Envious quick glances on the shameful intimacy
of the food going into her mouth.

Followed by burning embarrassing blush
From her inquiring eyes:

To finally land on the beginnings
of the involuntary grimace
Between joy and pain of her still glistening lips.

Swirl of meaningless plans and timetables into a future
Purposefully and humanly cut off from the present.

Akin to an emotional amputation to preserve… Not life or survival,
But more critically and longer lasting…
Dignity.

A last supper, with no godly input,
In which the coming stigmata would bleed very human
But nevertheless precious memories.

Dignity… that ethereal and yet concrete force.
The only one capable of stopping his begging for one more embrace
As a reaction to an imperceptible deep sigh.

His ultimate image in her eyes,
Keeping his forward movement away from her on the torrid sidewalk.

One last glance toward her.
Strange synesthesia in the ambient warmth
Of the residual heat from invisible flames of a picture album.

A contemporary and modernized reconstruction of many scenes of literature and films of a mutually unverbalized lovers' farewell. This time taking place in the incongruous fertility of a university coffee house.

The Perfume of the Gods

And the high priests of Egypt decreed perfumes to be the language of the gods

It seemed as though all the objects around her
had been laid out according to an immemorial protocol.

All the asymptotes from the universe of happiness
appeared in front of his mesmerized glance:

Anticipation and pleasure,
Longing and satisfaction,
Embrace and void.

Irritation and explosion,
A revisit and exhaustion.

Tonight and tomorrow morning,
The quieting quivers of satiation and the wrinkling of sheets.

The room was akin to a precious never seen Greek temple
built and immediately destroyed to its base
by an omnipotent selfish dreamer

Wanting its very existence to thus enter the domain
of the mythology of future lovers.

All this and other things rushed to his mind,
As wisps of the acrid sweetness of incense and floral burners
were carried over her nude body by the Mediterranean breeze.

Wild reconstructions of museums nudes invaded
his feverish eyes burning from sleeplessness and passion,

Transforming his standing at the foot of the minuscule bed
And the ghostly night traffic around the Place Clichy,

Into a splendidly hallucinogenic synesthesia
of religiosity and unbridled sensuality.

Emotion Recollected in Tranquility*

"Though nothing can bring back the hour of splendor in the grass, glory in the flower, we will grieve not; rather find strength in what remains behind."
                                                                William Wordsworth

Putting a period at the end of the poem
—A printer's trick to turn off a switch—
He had come back to his place in front of the screen.

Having left the comfortable other side
Where artistic tranquility exists.

He had now only what the artist has left on this side:
His mind and passion…
With only aftertastes of what seemed to always have been:
That presence in his arms

That breathing, those shallow breaths,
Those hints of her spasms like ripples of an inner vision.
A look into an alternate world… Another reality… Another dimension,

While furiously re-constructing the edifice to those fragile moments:
With and within the verbal universe of his poetry.

―――――――――――

Now back on the side of noisy reality:
She was indeed gone.

He had to remind his fingers of this harshness,
As hard as they were trying to deny it:
Using words, imagery, scents and reconstructed pliable flesh.

Gone… it was long gone
And yet living… There!... Between the left and right margins.

Art and the artist
Had rendered alive things that had been dead or dying:
Through the cold chemistry of intonation, onomatopoeias, metaphors.
Phraseology… Tools from a wise and studious past.

While on the side of alchemy,
They had known moment full of wormholes…
In a treasured recess known only to the two of them.

Outside of God… beyond any God:
Seen as no more than an absentee landlord.

But rather
Giving its role to the great hero of this drama:
The real and ultimately most important character,
In this aesthetic ménage à trois:
The future reader…

Where the only continuity that counts…. Exists.

Like the bending of space and time in the presence of black holes,
A forgiving Time allows lovers to bend the molecules of our will
To the grand monotheistic authority

That rewards lovers who have had their tender intimate moments
Etched on that Sinai granite mount.

* *"Poetry is the spontaneous overflow of powerful feelings: it takes its origin from emotion recollected in tranquility." In* Lyrical Ballads *by William Woodworth*

Also inspired by the Nausea *by Jean-Paul Sartre, an atheistic philosopher not known for his warmth, he writes that his future readers are his only claim to any equivalent of eternal life.*

From Both Sides of the Canvas

Nature Morte aux grenades et figues *

Surface texture, smelling of life itself.
Wavelets of contrasts, defined in shades of timid green,
Broken by the telling sanguinity of slashes.

Vertical pulpous vegetable flesh,
Hinting at concave treasures hidden under the engorgement of tactile pleasures,
Found in waiting lips dripping with an immanent taste of happiness.

The artist's pliable touch of the finest brush… and brushing,
Somehow magically recreated once again for our intimate understanding,

As we witness the grandiose moment of convergence,
On both sides of the canvas,

Between these two moments in space and time…

The tearful… Frozen… And still envious glance of the artist
And his generous invasion of ours… Standing in awe.

* *By Pierre-Auguste Renoir (1841-1919)*

In Lieu of a Painting

Splattering intimacy with searing adjectives:

Pliable phraseology… with the undulations and contortions of sensual explosions.

Recreating the pulsing sounds in their counter-point movements:
Somehow imitating the contact of lips against the ardor of passion.

Insertion of alternate guttural consonants
Full with the vowel-fluidity of acquiescence.

Ebullition of the genesis of life and its future starry swirls,
Under the disciplined control of the artist.

Seemingly limitless expanse of organic lubricity,
Helped by the translucence of edgy adverbs:

Giving the imagery of the sheen of life on quivering flesh.

Translation of the visceral morphology of sensuality
Into its human equivalents.

Making palpable,
What was, for a glorious instant, solely visual.

All the while, existed inside the verbal structure,
An intra-textual richness ready to combust into an alchemic transformation.

It would re-hydrate magically…
The distant mechanical sound of Parisian traffic…
The noble twist of the hips…
A hint of desire, expectation and of abandonment…

… Within the details of the description of a slight discernable pout
Seen in the filtered light from faded cheap curtains.

Verbal nobility
Giving an inestimable value to the humble setting,
That would make Renoir force his arthritic fingers to reach for the most inflamed red on his palette:
Echoing Courbet's unflinching statement of the carnality of life.

The moment and the subject,
Now posing for immortality as part of a religious voyeurism
For some future university student in a monastic room.

The artist through his art having finally transmuted the acrid smell of beads of sweat,
As they run over the marbly white flesh,
To then finish its flow into sanguine folds of reality.

A poet's equivalent of a painter's majestic nude rendition of a lover or muse in order to immortalize her or him for posterity.

Inner Sanctum

Reconstructing Paris

Let the notes gently glide in beads of softness over her taunt muscles:
Titillating right hand and sighs from the white keys.

Pulsating left… with no pity:
Rather invigorated by the gentle whimpered pain of friction.

Splendid display of abandonment to the rites of ecstasy.
Echoes from all the corners of the darkened room kept within their
intimate universe.

Her grimacing dominating glance of approval looking regally down
Through a black tangled forest of hedonism,

Linking to his own bewildered one
And a widening opening unto a spectacular crimson,

Leading to his realization
That the gods must have somehow mistakenly chosen him
For a rare taste and frustrating feminine glimpse
Into their most cherished selfish privileges.

To the music of TAO Lounge 4 "In the mood" by Monte la rue.

Reflected Gaze

A walk through a museum: Homage to Caravaggio

It is later in life
When your better friends have used you,
Her undying love-whispers evaporated,

Your favorite secret meeting place…

The one with the initials in the deep-veined wood,
Benign objects of life and living…

…Having become sources of tears.

That truths…
Somehow manage to reveal themselves
In the gaunt glance in your morning mirror,
Along with replays of the previous night's confession.

It is then…
In a masochistically yet pleasurable way,
That you find your double-ganger reflection
In that image of tortured soul-mate with your
haggard glance of misery,

Immerging from the violent chiaroscuro on a museum wall.

"You are afraid of yourself that is all. Like everyone. Me too, Harriet also… the wonderful little Andrea… Caravaggio. We are afraid of ourselves and of what we perceive of us in others."

[Author's translation* from the French version of Les chaussures ialiennes *by Henning Mankell*

[*Tu as peur de toi, c'est tout. Comme tout le monde. Moi aussi, Harriet aussi, la merveilleuse petite Andréa, le Caravage… Nous avons peur de nous-mêmes et de ce que nous apercevons de nous chez les autres.]

The Nobility of Moral Frailty

In Homage to François Villon, Caravaggio. Alfred de Musset and Charles Baudelaire

Glorifying awe,
Where others would see sin.

The perfume of the gods,
Where others would perceive debauchery.

Screams of ecstasy
And not anguish.

The face of a Madonna,
Where would otherwise lie depraved abandoned youth.

The warm oily scent of a tropical port,
Instead of carnal sweat.

Religious apotheosis…
Transmutation of pliable flesh,
where others would see the gates of Hell.

The beauty of Lucifer,
Instead of his jealous envy.

The need for the immediate beatitude of earthly happiness,
Where others would seek the promises of eternal salvation.

These artists: chosen for the tragic convergence and poetic result in their souls of the on-going battle between the attraction of purity and corruption in their personal lives.

Sanctuary

No gothic-beauty setting:
Instead off-green linoleum tiles
And cinder block-walled sub floor.

Anonymous dormitory
In endlessly repeated emotional skirmishes of university life.

Another mixer.
Another chance at a glimpse into those strange creatures.
Those co-eds that had peopled his Saturday night hours.

The mundane of the immemorial.
The stepping stones and the glorious missteps to falling in love.

He had not come in on a horse.
Not a knight in sight in this sorry overheated basement.

But here she was again… Abandoned on her seat:
Used and abused and yet still submissively willing to suffer the ritual.

Both now near the punch bowl,
Circling like two clueless moths.

Giving uneasy furtive inquiring glances.
Hints of empty arms over her empty embrace.
Heaving sighs revealed under heaving flowered dress.

Purported accidental and yet evincible tentative touch,
While her ex-boyfriend is fully immersed in his latest conquest.

Her pride shredding in synchronized time
At the rate of the birdlike palpitations of her breathing.

Glance of some internal panic in her.
Seconds and minutes are magically lost to the
coldness of an alchemic universe…

She now appears in his arms,
Falls in his arms… Falters in them.

Not embracing her…but rather keeping her on her feet,
Along with the ethical weight of this intimate drama,

He is trying to keep this gentle entity from unraveling.

Somehow this girl…This soul… This person,
Has entered him… Possessed him through her squeezing:

Looking for some sanctuary,
As though his arms acted the part of arches
of a cathedral's massive columns:
Thus offering her emotional survival.

Nothing glorious… No shining knight
Just sweeping up the modern-time spoils of love.

Iconic university party where male undergraduate ends up dancing with the abandoned ex-girlfriend of his buddy: Her, practically hanging on to him, out of sheer heartbreaking despair. Him, in this incongruous setting, out of a sense of unexplainable chivalry.

Tremors From the Universe

Their bodies had opened:
No suspicious restraint… Rather unconcerned abandonment.

Long…. Very long before understanding.
Un-verbalized probes of nature,
Brushing of trusting instincts
With vague demands from a new world,
Facing puzzled answers.

He… recalls the appropriately symbolic African heat.
Privacy among the rock-hard muddy shade.
Minimal clothing and minimal defenses.

Then a playful crouch among the spiny extensions
of prickly desert leaves,
Rubbing against reddening buttocks:
Electrical jumpstart of things to come.

She… was bathed
In the innocence of quiet playtime with doll:
Sleepy lavender summer afternoon.
Favorite doll in various dresses.

Unyielding neck line of miniature blouse
Tiny feet accidentally pushing on inner thighs.

Confused sensations.
Stellar explosions… Genesis of future instants:

Readying both bodies
In unblinking pensive awe of nature's fertile generosity.

A couple intertwined on a wrinkled bed inquiring from each other about their first remembered recollection of sexual sensuality in their youth: Both recalling having been involved in situations that startled their respective budding pubescence.

Jean-Yves, outside the walls of the Chella fortress in Salé, Morocco. This is near the site of Sidi Moussa, which will have an iconic presence in his work.

Tremors of the Universe II

She saw their presence on this bed, in this room,
    As the inevitability of their destinies.

While in his world, reigned chaos-theory:
    Blind forces bouncing off haphazard walls.

Hence this miraculous embrace… In time and space…
    The result of vapors of darkness pushing feathers at will.

Making her boyish slander body and sunlit smile,
    With the budding adult transfixing glance:

Toes gingerly touching the still cold wavelets of a New England beach,

And his cute short pants and squinting shyness in the African heat,

That much more evidence of the generosity

--The gift… from an otherwise unfeeling universe--

For having brought these two youngsters together:
    In this… the iconic sounds of human happiness,

In a random corner of a deaf cosmos.

A couple intertwined on a wrinkled bed, looking at respective family photographs of themselves as youngsters.

II

THE REPLACEABLE SOLIDER

The Replaceable Soldier

French Resistance fighter meets "America" in the incarnation of a tall G.I. walking from the Fréjus landing.

He first appeared in the sulfurous fumes of Freedom
with incongruously scented herbes-de-Provence undertones.

Tall lanky Kansas milk-fed giant
smelling of Lucky Strikes and sporting an endless perfect white smile.

Like all great apocalyptic arrivals,
He was preceded by end-of-days deluges.
End-of-times curtains of incendiary bombs
with well-meaning chess-game, amoral destruction of cartloads of tired
potato-farming field-hands

Meeting the imminent end of their lives
next to expressionistic sunflowers.

This quasi-mythological mechanized force... from "over there"...
This apparently new breed of "our" very own descendants.

Descendants of those who had passed under the torch of Lady Liberty
In the bleary hours of a New World.

These... 'Children of our children', who had multiplied and
prospered in a Star-Trek-way
Had come back to help...
Only to face the entanglement of sadistic satisfaction:

The infliction of local justice on the burnt breast nipples
of 'collaboratist' office secretaries.

Months and years latter...
These horrible memories and images
had been tightly packed behind them,

The remains of the French family dashes...
No... Escapes toward the even warmer sun of the Maghreb.

Far away... Far as possible away
from the haunting reminders of bullet and shrapnel holes
'poxed' into the sacred and bleached columns of
Greek and Roman temples:

Modern viral residues of embedded scars
that refuse to dissolve into the Mediterranean blue laced marble.

A dash... To the edge of the roar of the Atlantic
that had previously stopped the very westward flow of Islam,

Within sight of a miniscule beach
and into the welcoming nonjudgmental arms
of the Marabout Sidi Moussa,
the protector of infertile women.

A setting at the earthly border of the Moorish empire...
'The setting sun", the Maghreb.

At the feet of the Kasbah Udayas. The Other... becoming the Other...

A place of respite... a visual and sensual pot-pourri
of ethnicities and beliefs.
Multi layered taste of pungent cumin and honeyed pastries

Boiling minted tea...
Somehow turning into masochistic pleasure in the ambient torrid heat.

Hypnotic drum beats and wild fantasias on frantic yet obedient white
Arabian stallions.

Could this exotic setting be an illusion rendered believable and more real
by the magic of the quieting balm it imposed on these ugly...
much too real wounds?

Unfortunately... like these tales
told to sleepy children everywhere and anywhere:

Such as in smoky African huts, brittle ice cold nights of Scandinavia, or under organic Scottish wool,

... It is hinted to youth
In these so-called fantastic fables, in gentle, yet unyielding ways

That truths,
Do eventually hurt and scar by the nature of their truths:

Adults having, long ago, tearfully
Learned to accept that the boogey man, the big bad wolf
Were indeed under the bed:

And Santa Claus long ago
Too tired, disillusioned and having forsaken his appearance at the stroke
of midnight, to come undo our mistakes.

And so it happened, on a beautiful day
at a wildly untamed beach at the mouth of the muddy Oued Sebou,

The giver of more than its share of precious
inner -land fresh water to the greenish ocean,
On a wind-swept hill...
full of synesthesia recreated by the 'echoing smells'
of the maritime pines,

That this man... now with his son gripping his huge hand,
Climbed up this hill in endless Sisyphus fashion...
again and still feverish with the same human pain and human sorrow
found in the dark recesses of his life caused by living.

This man and his son stood silently in swirls of pathetic fatigue,
In front of a tiny American cemetery of gigantic importance,
With alignments of the tombs of GIs who had
previously left their parents
Quietly crying their evaporating futures on the cement steps of a
Brooklyn tenement,

In order for their own son to repeat the rite of passage
of the replaceable soldier.

> Their son... Flesh of their flesh... Having now taken his turn
> To fight and die in the rich earth of, by now,
> disinterested multiple gods.

Thoughts about war and events surrounding the arrival of Allied troops on the Côte d'Azur in France in August '44 following the Normandy landings; as well as the one in Morocco (November '42) where is located, high up on a hill overlooking the beach of Mehdia, a lesser known tiny American cemetery.

A Voice From Company C 4th Platoon

The setting seemed more than appropriate:
Cold wind-driven snow filtering through broken window.

Just the incongruous warmth of quasi-strangers,
In the strangeness of olive drabs,
Thrown in the mixer of military experiment.

There existed a richness of language,
A mix of eclectic expressions
And some genuine hilarious misunderstandings,
Pushing back momentarily the ambient shadows.

But there was a universally understood
Sarcastic sadness in the tone of someone on the corner footlocker:

"They should draft the rich first:
They have more to lose then the kids in my neighborhood."

Conversation of a group of Viet Nam War draftees sitting in company barracks.

A Successful Life

In homage to "Amédée, or How to Get Rid of It" by Eugène Ionesco.

A man with an excellent image.
The kid who had done well.

Even the iconic football trophies,
To go with eventual trophy cheerleader-wife:

A blessed human being on all levels.

Amazingly not beyond showing interest
in the lesser beta-males of his entourage:

Definitely a "man's man"

Guilt comes to us à la carte:
We can choose the parts we want to ignore,
Leaving it in the kitchen.

But like the unrelenting odor
of that particularly nauseating spice going by our table,

after all these years… a media report too many,
… a teen-age son in his life,

lead to the unsolicited admission:

"My draft deferment was bogus… I didn't go."

Chance conversation with neighborhood school friend with an apparently spotless and successful life.

Rorschach Inkblot Test

Multi-layered anxiety.
Hard-hat signs of encouragement.
Peace sign by guitar-playing hippy.

Unhidden hilarity
Of teen-age girls, at pathetic appearance.
Teary tender smile
From grandmother whose grandson he resembles.

This uniform guarantees no anonymity:
Seemingly reflecting the mood of a nation.

The goal is simply to make the bus to Virginia:
And the Army green is more like a red flag.

Reflecting whatever people,
Their questions… beliefs… anger… sadness…
Want to read into it.

Little do they know,
That every one of their varied and contradictory feelings
Exist in the merciful uniformity of the cloth:
Hiding his pounding heart.

Walking through New York City bus terminal circa 1968 in U.S. Army private uniform.

Rising From the Mud

1914-2014

It was her…
Always present whenever he missed her.
It was her…
Her floral perfume and flowing dress
The one she had worn for the fair
It was her…
Ethereal and soft... Musical and moist.
It was her…
Incandescent and reserved... Pastoral and misty:

Rising in immaculate vestal whiteness,
Miraculously untouched by the mud that had given her birth.

Twenty year old looking at the sky from the no-man's land of World War One, as he lies dying.

A Beautiful Baby

1914-2014

Grand child for a new century.
Village in land of plenty.

Plump chickens and velvety milk.
Ordered life of hard working people,
In multi-generational households.

No luxuries and no vacations:
Instead, sleepy Sunday sermons from well-meaning priest;
Boisterous drinks at local bar,
Over rumors of some price hikes for Alsatian coal.

The boring routine of endless cycles of routine:
While sturdy farmhouse walls somehow kept the outside out
And the inside continuous.

Hints of military unrest and patriotic demands
Scoffed at... as unnatural interference with the grape harvest.

Grand child of the new century
Destined to marry the gentle seamstress
And become the master of the known world…

… All the way down to the stone wall border,
By the crooked tree with disappearing lovers' initials
And not beyond.

A day came that took that grandchild away
And sent him to a hell hole of shredded youthful flesh.

She could see... she could feel...
She could still touch... his fingers that had fingered
The innocence of the white nectar of the first milking of the day:
Inorganic grayish-white fingers… now frozen on a rifle trigger.

She could somehow hear her name on his lips...
The way he would whimper during an earache.

The way the brittle shiver of late autumn leaves
          Foretells their winter death.

French grandmother's world devastated by the news of her grandson's death in the carnage of World War One.

Through a Child's Eyes

November 1942: the German Axis occupies the rest of Vichy France.

These were not happy times for a seven year old little girl:
Winter was setting in: even in Southern France.

More gray than usual,
The clouds seemed to have known something.

But her mother was a miracle worker:
The butcher having served according to grown-ups priority,
His rich clients, politicians and his mistress,

The bones and meager shreds of meat would make a thin ragoût;
The watered wine would suffice daddy,

And, maybe with curtains drawn, door locked and coffee made
of mixture of roasted chestnuts skins:
An illusion of surrealistic quietude could reign?

The parents had done what parents do:
Make bad things stop at the door.

Until that afternoon… and the grayish loaf of bread
missing from mother's basket.

And the little girl's tearful return with coins still in her hand,
Returning from the baker:
"Mommy… the baker told me that there is no more bread!"

Inspired by a true event for a seven-year old growing fast and understanding, better than children should, the concept of war at the human level.

Through a Child's Eyes II

To a learned goat, who must have been reading the headlines.*

Sunday pastries after church and apéritif at the bistrot de la gare,
Now things of the past.

Along with the running joke in the household:
Of all the adults on a State-imposed slimming diet.

Coq au vin had disappeared with the demise of the rooster.
But the nanny goat up on the other side of the village
had been a life-saver:

Somehow, cow-milk intolerance not impressed by things of the world.

It was, reportedly, in a solemn voice that the farmer announced
the cut-back in his animal's production:

Seemingly condemning the toddler to colicky nights.

Screaming news papers headlines and pompous political speeches,
Proclamations of travel protocols and military campaigns,

Emotional and physical agonies drown out the sounds of his pain.

So no one ever heard.
Perhaps… they should have.

* *Paraphrased comment attributed to the child's father.*
Occupation of Vichy France, circa fall 1942.

A Higher Wall and Different Color

All will be fine now in the great temple of illusions:
The preparations in place.
The candles lit and the incense burning.

Soft lighting and sweetly acrid smoke,
Permeating the now more dignified space.

High priests and priestesses,
Proceeding with complete respect and adoration in their eyes:
Bowing, kneeling and praying in clocklike unison.

The gods will be pleased as they look down favorably
On our need for keeping patriotic face.

Nothing like the vapors of appearances and humiliation
To change the gritty reality of the solid world.

Nothing like rituals and make-belief,
To give… to make-belief… more believability.

The sacred oils and sincere hymns,
Will give henceforth more gravitas and meaning

To the blood curdling shrieks of the young soldier from Cleveland
During his private time with death.

"From the moment the design is publicized, a small group within the Vietnam Veterans' community felt Lin's statement was an affront." [PBS WGBH]

About the original design of the Vietnam War Memorial Wall being criticized by some as visually, militarily or patriotically too timid.

A Saintly Father

Family gatherings when past issues are revisited

A time for family gathering:
Sprinkled with the reappearance of uncles and cousins.

Overwhelming embraces from buxom aunts
Joyous indulgence of overindulgences.

Fertile chaos of familial heated conversations…
And especially the expected anticipation
Of the night's purpose:

The midnight arrival of le Père Noël,
Along with his obligatory entrance ticket… the gifts.

He would occasionally still lie awake as an adult,
With echoes of these pivotal evenings,

When loud accusatory words about black market coupons
Reached his bedroom door,
Conflated with his father's distributing toys under the tree

That led to the double death of an irreproachable image
And the evaporation of Santa Claus.

Inspired by the novel **Dora Bruder** *by Patrick Modiano when the narrator is thinking about his father's ethical contamination during his survival in occupied France during World War II.*

Shrapnel of Love

As though the very gentleness of the colors
Had always been meant to disgrace… by their dignity,
The horror of the sight.

The tender fragility of the paper.
The powdery protection of the plaster.
The strewn disincarnated undergarments.

Collapsed night table.
A hanging suitcase: stopped in mid-flight:
Gapping hole into a private drama.

A public statement for all to be witnesses
Of the secret passion that once reverberated within these walls.

And in spite of the screams of the wounded and dying,
The whispers of ecstasy and half-syllables of pleasure
Were still echoing within those unspoiled moments of mankind
When some of our most natural emotions
Are played in the sinless world of lovers.

A contrasting display that shames us,
In front of this privileged spot:
On this earth… This city… And life.

A place of so much happiness,
Now blanched by the sterilizing rays of the sun.

Bombing air raid survivor recognizing the wall paper of the bedroom of the destroyed hotel where he and a colleague had known splendid hours.

Personal Conscience and Collective Absolution.

Worse and more shameful wars had been and would be fought.

Even the causes were reasonably honorable.
The blind mechanisms of evils seemingly aligned all on one side.

The personae properly evil looking:
Thick wire-rimmed glasses from pathological beings.

Ridiculously small mustache and guttural Teutonic overtones
from a denatured universe.
Goose-stepping energy of high jacked cultural symbols.

A veritable gift from the war gods to the future chapters of Veterans of Foreign Wars, in the microcosm of Americana.

Gory details from inebriated old soldiers:
Feeling their oats once more with a shot of whiskey-inducement.

It would be understandable to ignore a quiet costumer
on the far end of the bar,
Still dealing with very live ghosts of otherwise good men
Wearing very bad uniforms:

Dying—in front of his glassy glance—very painful muddy deaths
from eviscerated organs.

"I would cry myself to sleep each night for what I had done during the day and know that I would have to do it again the next day." [From an infantry soldier fighting his way from the Normandy beaches in the early days of the landings in Normandy]

Fictional reconstruction from a recollection of a soldier based on Andrea Shae N.P.R. interview on June 6, 2014.

Convergence

Stomach still grumbling after meager rice and invisible protein meal.
Infected wound on left ankle.
Quasi delirious state of sleepwalking.

Kalashnikov and M-16 having replaced
Respective sleeping mates at their sides
Since leaving the gentle swaying of reeds
And brittle swirling snows.

Fresh baby face and ascetic glance.
Furtive mirror images opposite muddy river bank.

Conscripts losing their patriotic zeal
At the rate of mosquito bites,
Exploding green patches,
The milking of water buffalo,
The fickle high school sweetheart,
The burden of a seventh child,
The prophecies of Bob Dylan,
The boredom of indoctrination,
The indiscriminate violence of pacification

And the vaporous… Amoral…
Repetitive numbness of killing, for both.

All of that and much more came to an end
When the target, the end of the rifle
And the pull of the trigger…
Converged

And one of the mirror image
Would sleep the sleep of so many before him:

Never knowing the haggard glances of home.

The lives of a Vietnamese military conscript and his American counterpart intersect mortally in the jungle circa 1968

The Human Face on Destiny

Intelligence officer's ultimate existentialist decision

He was known as the Pyramid:
Nothing or no issue could shake him.

His very presence gave grounding and meaning to his men:
No matter how ephemeral or hopeless the situation.

The sort of officer that would require Hollywood
no less than a Robert Mitchum to incarnate.

He seemed to always have a smiling squint:
Leading his men to believe everything would be just fine in the long run.

Little did anyone appreciate the lethal human agony
He brought to his bunk after his rounds,

Having sealed in the safe the list of broken-code information
That would not be divulged and not sent to shipping out at sea.

As burning phantasmagoric visions
Would play through his tears on the cold metal of his locker.

Inspired, with poetic license, by World War II documentary on submarine warfare and the need to keep Allies Enigma code-breaking from becoming obvious to the Nazis. It is thus implied that some ship traffic was knowingly put in danger.

Historical Monument:
3rd Quarter of Twentieth Century*

Clarity…
Blinding clarity of physical location

Clear-eyed purpose.
Unwavering intransigence of sculptural ethics:

The architect. The crypt. The decrees and by-laws.
The third quarter of the twentieth century it specifies.

Historic monument for the betterment of world artistic estate.
Words and personalities.
Presidents and coalitions of support.

Eternal flames of remembrance.

All of it on a little corner of an island.
On the tip of that island known from time immemorial
Since the fishing days of the Parisii

As an apparently and eternally special place.

Now bathed in an incongruous urban silence:
Not unlike the one that welcomed the cries of mothers
On those inhumane hours.

---

* Unsentimental bureaucratic language describing this heart wrenching monument. Author's translation of the official descriptive declaration by the French government and the city of Paris of the monument of remembrance to the mass arrests of French Jewish families: It is at the tip of l'ile de la Cité, next to Notre Dame de Paris.

Multiple Realities

"I'm so sorry… I can't honestly commit to anything." *

The passion of the conversation somehow made
the frigid New England night irrelevant,

While an asthmatic sixties-Volkswagen's heater did its best to make it so.

A world and its bounty in his arms.
A tomorrow morning and its pleasures sweetly acquired.
:
Indeed the best of the best beginnings of all possible worlds.

Until the reptilian nature of the heart-breaking nature of his words
Seemed to bounce off her green eyes back unto his soul.

Precious moments when the world and its futures
Were still gapingly opened in his arms.

A time when two self-excluding solemnities still co-existed
In incestuous disgust in his own heart:
Revealing insidious flaw lines in his happiness.

All the while his universe was all there… inches away,
In the gentle searching crease of her gaze,
In the hint of an upward grimacing slant of her lips:

His words were now bouncing off a rising sea of green.

Playing the role of a Greek chorus
The crumpled Selective Service letter in his jacket
Would sound a reminder every time she would rest
her blond hair on his chest….

At night's end, he turned once more toward her
as she walked to her dorm,

Making him grapple with the existentialist silence
of his gesture many years later,
Along with the fragility of the dividing line
between our multiple realities.

* *Pivotal words from recently drafted university student.*

Inspired by the play "Si on recommçait?"[What if we could do it over again?] by Eric-Emmanuel Schmitt:

Alex returns to the home of his youth. Through a strange phenomenon, he finds himself facing his past, during a crucial day. Forty years later, he meets again the young women he had desired, his grandmother whom he loved, and maybe himself... Would he make the same choices now that he knows what became of his life?
(Translation of online outline of play)

Of Gypsies, Jews and Others

There was no presence of sharp-edged desert stones,
Cutting into unsteady sandaled feet.

Nor the divine heat of a divine sun nullifying any hiding cool shade
That would dare hide universal truths.

This Messianic exodus
To the place of revelation was a different rite of passage:
It was darkened
By the absence of any protective enlightened prophetic glance.

Fathers
Instead… playing the role of helpless consolers.

Mothers
Protecting… their children with the emaciated strength of their love.

Leaving, as the only purifyingly cleansing fire,
The fires of the final solution:

With some of the nourishing flesh having been previously refused
A righteous and simple human claim:

Its own place of nightly rest.

Inspired by Patrick Modiano's novel "Dora Bruder" and the deportation of Jewish families from France by German and French Vichy authorities during the occupation.

"Ils ont toujours habité dans une chamber d'hôtel" [They always lived in a hotel room]. A reference to the Bruder family as having lived in hotel rooms from their marriage date to their deportation.

Sleepwalkers of World War I

In a schoolyard of Europe circa first decade of 1900's

Robust carefree abandonment of energy.
Shouts of youth in the chirping chaos of a schoolyard.

Sly taunting, pushing and shoving.
Scatological insults aimed at ancestry and family members.
Protective friendships in smart exchange for lunch time peace.

Religions, tastes, mannerism and skin tones,
Mindlessly criticized.

In extremis,
Potential black eyes and ripped shirt avoided
By benevolent observing parental glance of teachers.

If only this cocoon of quaint childhood Lilliputian worries
Could have existed on the grander scale
In the soporific somnolence of the Belle Époque,
To prevent the mindless shredding of real flesh
In the mud trenches of history:

Creating over the playground… phantasmagoric shadows
Of crying schoolboys astonished
At their prophetic future pain of physical violence.

Nobody at the time called the assassination of Archduke Franz Ferdinand in Sarajevo on June 28, 1914, "a shot heard round the world." The phrase, filched from Ralph Waldo Emerson's "Concord Hymn," epitomizes a judgment that crystallized only as the horrendous sequels played out. Some parts of the international community weren't listening at all. America was serene in its isolation and prosperity. "To the world, or to a nation," The Grand Forks Herald in North Dakota declared, "an archduke more or less makes little difference." President Wilson, pacing the lonely corridors of the White House, was distraught over the first lady's failing struggle for life. Paris was engrossed in a murder trial brimming with sex and political scandal. London was too obsessed with Irish home rule to sustain attention until closer to midnight.
The Sleepwalkers: How Europe Went to War in 1914, *By Christopher Clark*

The Train Engineer*

The improbability of remaining innocent in the omnipresence of evil

The calluses on his hands
Could not insulate his conscience.

His flesh knew full well, through the emptiness of the cold,
Where its sisters' flesh had been sent.

In the universality of right and wrong,
Behind the petrified glances of children,
Awash in the non-humanity of so-called fellow humans,

Remained the witnesses:
The human organic residues… on the soiled floor boards
of the cattle cars;
The child's shoe… the torn handkerchief… the broken tooth…
The picture… of a happier little boy on a carousel horse.

Those unspoken atoms of dignity… distilled to this repulsive imagery,

When humanity reduces to cinders the absolute miracle
That should be celebrated through its very unlikely existence.

So… it was spoken, by the spoon…
To this otherwise honorable man and trembling fingers…

As he felt tortured by his daughter's unspoiled smile.

* *The French railways recognized its complicity after the war.*

The solid hands of hard working man tremble as they "recognize," in the metallic coldness of the soup spoon, the similar cold as the one of the control lever of the locomotive he had brought in the previous morning to the gates of the concentration camp of Dachau.

"But We… We Didn't Do Anything Wrong"*

Reciprocal glances between passing souls,
On opposite sides of an opening chasm:

A school court-yard on one side.
And angular barbed-wires of the Shoah on the other.

Divergent destinies:
One of forced return to the boredom of parental control;
The other, bewildering growls of dogs and spot-lights.

The weight of inhumanity on young shoulders.
Or the bothersome delayed lunch on the other.

Led to die with the glance of the Other's glance upon them
Which, both will carry
Along with their last remnants of human dignity,

Having known some solidarity in facing the face of Evil.

This courtyard, akin to the stage of a Greek tragedy:
With, however, no fickle Olympian gods to blame.

The Chorus of young classmates,
Forced to accept a sort of tragic flaw:

Exhibited in the evidence of innocence of soul,
Through an intact foreskin.

---

* "*Nous… n'avons rien fait… nous*" : *Reaction of a non-Jewish student stating his innocence in front of his classmates and the German soldiers there to arrest their three friends with false papers: For him, their Jewish status is guilt enough and their problem: In addition to which, he is always looking toward lunch.*

Reflection on the iconic scene of Louis Malle's Au revoir les enfants *when the three Jewish students are denounced and taken away in front of the rest of their classmates.*

Between the Jehovah Witness and the S&M Prostitute

To the women of Ranvensbrük

Place of obscene contrast.
Place of nobility of conduct.
A place of haughty rebellion in shredded cotton dresses.
The pliable strength of resilience.

Lost cause.

Sisterhood within the universe of gratuitous perversion.
Selfless actions that help us redefine the human
In the vile waters of inhumanity.

Symbols of mankind's maternal icons,
In the frigid shadows of fascism.

Eternal dignity of fixed glance of survivors,
As stern witnesses of inenarrable moments
Fixed for posterity in the sternness of the camera.

Beautiful femininity in all of them,
Contradicting the hideous specters behind the barbed-wires.

A place of extremes.
Of eternal grandeur of the message.
Of mortified and degraded flesh.
Giving birth… life springing for this hole of death:
Contradicting the moment for the moment.

Mothers, sisters. Whores and academics.
All doing their part in the grandiose dignity and self-respect.

And from the urban sex trade,
The unequal ironic stand of a dominatrix
Refusing orders to beat her inmate sisters.

From the unspeakable horrors of the Ranvensbrük women concentration camp during World War II came examples of the nobility of human defiance from all parts of society.

III

ART AND REALITY

Trailways* Idyll

The ambiance was artificially cooled:
The oppressive outside humidity controlled by freezing flow
from hidden ducts.

The enlisted basic-training stripes were not impressive;
Nor was the double strangeness of the sub-culture of a new culture.

But the half-whispered apology for an errant knee
Must have sounded like an existentialist statement of beliefs.

A gentle stream of innocuous words
Played the part of a soothing balm,

Turning the accidental hint of her elbow
Into a revelation of secretive acquiescence.

Emotions…
Have a way of ignoring the laws of space and time,
So the transport…
To a very urban diner's table was seamless.

―――――――――――――――――――――――

… Something about the next time and place to meet
Were the last civil thoughts that he would associate with her.

Before the inhumanity of the words shouted at them
Burst the time capsule that they had or would ever live.

Chance meeting of white foreign-born Viet Nam war era conscript riding north to Washington D.C. with an Afro-American girl next to him. [Circa 1968]

*Trailways bus company

Cyrano: A Fable

He did not tower over people:
He could not.

Nor could his very presence
Sweep anything or anyone.

To even things, as it is want to do,
Nature had given him a discreetly generous soul.

He had a rare and spectacular ability to transform the space,
Inhabited all in turn by us in this universe,
Into something somehow more precious for having known him.

Like many constructs of fairytales,
He had an unpretentious innate nobility of soul
That presumed, in turn, everyone having an equal of his own:

In a world
Where valor and value are more often the stuff of the ephemeral
And the arbitrary codes of inert physical imagery.

As this fable would have it,
He had generously painted others around him
With pigments of his own brand of the beautiful.

And not unlike in too many of these tales,
In the end, the many were left with the nagging consciousness

That the world would have been a better place,
If more persons had suffered his surface imperfections.

A beautiful soul in less than beautiful body

A Place at the Table

What part of the Constitution explains my not being able to sit at this table?
[Non-attributed account of a returning black soldier to the Jim Crow South]

I did not sit down simply to have something to eat or drink.
I did not sit down expecting to get more than my part of the meal.
I did not sit down to gorge myself with sweets.

I did sit down to sustain what every man needs:
His part of human worthiness among other humans.

I did not crawl in the mud of battle
To ask permission for a velour seat.

I did not kill to preserve a concept of equality…
To be looking through the windows.

I did not earn these medals
To simply be allowed to serve coffee.

And I surely did not defend this flag
To find prisoners of war from the other
Taking my place at the table.

A Post-Modern Woman

There was an intriguing ambivalence about her:

Not in his immediate attraction to her.
Nor in his approval of her.

It was rather in the very complexity… The layering of her composition.

Her unconventional circuitry and avant-garde programation,
according to the computer guys' vocabulary.

But especially, in that reflection of his own masculinity
Hinted in her eyes.

All these and any other questions were answered,
As echoes of her gentle but firm confessional comment
Were still burning in his soul:
Along with the scalding taste of office coffee on his lips..

"I would not allow myself to be passively seduced.
In a losing position of inferiority,

I learned all
From his unrelenting and unstoppable aggression:

Using it to make him want me… to his own submissive
destruction."

Un-attributed comments by a particularly attractive, bright, single female employee about the misogynous world in which she had survived.

Androgyny

In homage to Auguste Rodin, The Metamorphosis of Ovid

She had overpowered him,
Through the simple passion in her glance.

An emotionally incestuous motherly reminder
Of his passive, obedient youth.

Her ascetic sternness transformed into a smile of quasi-beatitude
Often found in the marble of religious statues.

He retained an instinctive respect for her tastes
Thus not inquiring into her feminine virility.

Beside this domineering side
He had been privileged to see precious hints of her fragility,
Symbolized by an untouched blossoming beauty
Coupled to an extraordinary lubricity.

The whole, safeguarded in order to protect an intimate dignity.

She carried elemental pieces of a little girl
In whom was imprisoned a continuing ambivalence…

… Until apparently this kiss, this minute and second
When the solid edifice collapsed into a marbly powder.

He could only feel mesmerized:
As he submissively looked up at her nude silhouette
in the shadows of the curtains,
As she was letting herself go… akin to the gentle entrance of museum
muses into warm water.

He was imagining that the very bestial nature of their act
Offered a primary, primordial, reptilian glance on the past and future:

Like a giant elementary particle accelerator

The nuptial darkness of the room matched the blackness of creation:
Before culture and much before social graces.

The magical room became a setting immune to the artifice of mannerisms…
A place that preceded the invention of sin.

It seemed as though there existed a protecting overlay
Shielding them from everyday responsibilities:

Leaving them naked… face to face in a post paradisiacal world
calling her… calling him… calling them

At this precise time in her life, her flesh had resolved
That the laws of things and man could be or should be transgressed…

From the depth of her being… unverbalized feelings had been boiling
Causing her perceptible quivers of trepidation.

She became possessed by an irresistible urge towards… freedom…
fantasy…and dreams.

That is when he recognized that look in her…
It had existed in his!

It had been in his glance in the salt of a beach cave of Sidi Moussa
When the strangely innocent world of searching pubescence
appeared to a little boy

It had been his in the strange smoky moistness on the iced grass
of his teenage years.

It had been his in the thin-walled echoes of lubricity in a minuscule room
of the Saint Germain des Prés of Henry Miller.

It had been his in the midnight moon reflection off Greek gods statues
while overlooking Mont Sainte Victoire.

It had been his upon the entrance on an overheated dance floor and this unexpected receptive glance among the blinding lights.

She represented all of these things through her glance upon him
In which was captured unscripted human thoughts of joy
And the simmering jealousy of the gods.

Reflection on The Garden of Eden *by Hemingway and a reprise of some the corresponding themes from* Clair-obscur de l'âme *and* Clair-Obscur of the Soul.

Appetite and Disdain

Aberration of the soiling of intimacy,
With stains of
Denaturalization of the most iconic natural act.

Repulsive convergence,
In the minds of otherwise mild bureaucrats and respected businessmen,

Of inhuman…
No! Non-human* acts:

That of the unholy alliance
Of the expressed purpose of the splendor of this flesh
And the imposed violence upon it.

Double vision in the glance of the aggressor
Of desire... Disdain.
Appetite and yet revulsion.

Uncontrolled drive.
Hopelessness and true eternal obscenity.

While instead
Turning a very human act
Into a nihilistic gesture devoid of any claim to membership in humanity.

Sexual assault added to the abject misery of Jewish women during their "registration" at the hand of collaborating French and the German authorities during the Val d'Hiv round up in Paris 1942.** As well as the sexual gratification anticipated by their future white owners of female slaves being "processed" in such scenes as 10 Years a Slave.

* *Term used by Jorge Semprùn [i.e for whom 'inhuman' is a contradiction of terms]*
** *Dora Bruder by Patrick Modiano*

Art and Reality

"The poet is a liar who always speaks the truth." Jean Cocteau

In a world… where the viewer has the nagging feeling
Of detecting

… More truth about life and living…

In the surprisingly pungent seedy engorged sanguinity of languishing and tempting fig halves… of a nature morte,

Further followed by his oscillating, timid glance…

Between the humid charcoal forest of intimacy found in the pubic hairs
And that of the unblinking aggressive eyes of a reclining nude.
Found under the sheen of academic oils

A world with lies and hypocrisy usually hidden
Behind the boudoir respectability of sheer-silk cloth dividers

In a world…
That lives on both sides of the canvas,

Full of unexposed and unspoken excesses,
Varnished-over by the canons of Sunday worships,

Full with pseudo-pains of religious ecstasy
And clair-obscures delineating shades of immorality and peace of mind
As displayed by smirking Dutch money changers:
This viewer becomes a voyeur of his own voyeurism:

Art and the artist…
Unashamedly displaying rampant indecency
With its reptilian but only too human genesis.

Reflections on the apparent moral violence presented by the Paris Musée d'Orsay exposition "Sade: attaquer le soleil" as well as the immortal fertile bounty of Courbet's "The Origin of the World" and the real and more dangerous obscenity of the attacks at "Charlie Hebdo."

Silky Reality

What would a beautiful actress's skin look like under a microscope?

Seeing… as merely reconstructions:
A conspiracy of the necessary and the stable.

Of the intelligence of composition.
The substance of form.

Sight… evolving into the trickery of comfort
and of needed emotional deceit:

The sculptural waves of impressionistic nudes.
The wispy raspberry hue of Renoir's muses.
Manet's marbly-white impregnability of a woman's thigh.

Seeing solidity where exist merely photons,
Made of haphazard reflections.

The artist's superimposed inner landscape,
Over the harshness of realities of Things.

Reflection on the passage in Gulliver's Travels *where the minuscule hero is repulsed by the defects of the nursemaid's huge breasts; and the continued findings in neuro-science implying that human perception of the world is just that: perception; as well as artists' interpretations of their own reality.*

Billie Holiday and Édith Piaf

Of the lyricism of urban decay described by the art of Charles Baudelaire.

Improbable beauty of the flowers of evil,
Having found sustenance and strength in the organic filth
Spread negligently among the stained bed sheets.

Once girlish enthusiasm suppressed,
In the bruised intimate flesh.

Absence of kind words in shuttered spaces of unloving embraces,
Made of muscular aggressive appetites.

Maternal and paternal protective glances
Gone… Long gone into the darkest corners of neglect.

A whole world of youth and innocence turned up side down
By the adult calculus of unreturned self-satisfaction.

Listen…
Listen to the intonations.
Notice…
The vibrato of the throat.
Appreciate…
The phraseology of the sentiments.
Detect…
The heartbreaking imagery.

A trembling emaciated sparrow… A glistening charcoal-plumed bird:
Both somehow finding within the depth of nothingness,
When everything else had been taken away,

Finding… In the emptiness of emptiness,
The shreds of humanity that remain
When the electric sterility of the bright lights of the stage

Offer the only source of human warmth,
Momentary forgetfulness

And any possibility of hope,

As seen through the moist eyelids of personal misery
And well beyond the shadowy figures of the orchestra seats.

Billie Holiday and Édith Piaf: singers with eerily similar personal lives of early sexual abuse and their survival: all irremediably linked to an innate musical style and talent.

Stone Dust

He had always been in awe of this man:
A man's man by the account of other men and women.

Impeccably carrying the insignia of the old country's military:
Decorated and adulated by the neighbors.

Taller than tall,
In the iconic indigo well-fitted uniform.
An image of quiet solidity in polished boots.

Leather straps and side-arm,
With echoes of life and death past deeds.

Regally balanced by omnipresent smiling creased eyes
And quiet natural self-assured authority.

Just a father now,
Standing in the kitchen of the New World for supper.

With a sort of Mikado-mask of white dust
And filthy shoes:

Never having looked so handsome.

New immigrant teenager looking at his father, back from backbreaking first job in America, covered with stone dust.

Acculturation:
Sounds of Snapping Crust

Good flour, yeast, salt, water.
Touching tomorrows by its very momentary simplicity.

The loaf at the side of grand-father at the table head:
The immemorial position of honored positions for both.

Good flour, yeast, salt, water
Primordial oven and the perfume of life on earth.
Invading the street twice a day from sidewalk vents.

The baker and his wife, now with children gone,
Like fairytale parents, would continue creating magic.

Moments that still resonate today,
In the snapping of the golden crust.

In the respectfully secular, yet biblical grandeur, of
Good flour, yeast, salt, water.

Cultural memories that acquired the aura of quasi-religious gestures in a different culture: Southern French Baguette versus processed sliced white bread of New England.

French Kiss

Just a different modifier:
But a kiss should still be just a kiss. No?

The embrace started similarly.
After all, just a token of her affection and introduction to new culture.
"Do you know what it is here?"
…………..
Leaving one speechless.

Of learning the American version of a simple kiss: Teenager introduction to a new teenage world.

Madeleines

Cleaning out dad's belongings.

It was not the piles of boxes,
Haphazard papers of old pension stubs;
Return ticket from Paris.
Faded grammar school first prize ribbons

It was not even the embarrassingly personal items
Cloth-dryer-abused underwear and various ointments.

His son had shrugged off, with merely a hint of a smile,
The innumerable coupon cut-outs.
Buttons of all sizes and elastics in plastic bags

Plastic bags in plastic bags:
A spontaneous tension release of healthy laughter.

No… none of these pieces covered by a symbolic dust
Stopped the rhythm of drawer… packing box… screeching of packing tape.

All over sudden… A bolt… from another world and other time.
A paralysis of the body; but not the soul.

Selective blindness of peripheral vision:
White noise of heart beats blocking reality.

He would never be able to account for the length of time
It took the stool under him to travel to that church fair
Of his youth,

As he felt a warm wetness on his trembling hands
And the image of a beaming man
Behind a squinting little boy.

We all have our own "Madeleines"… sometimes it is just a faded black and white photograph.

Constructive criticism

Author's poetic inspiration based on Hemingway's retort to Scott Fitzgerald's 'constructive' critic of A farewell to Arms: *"Kiss my ass."*

Simply wanting to capture the vaporous nature of her hair.
The way the angle of her hips
Reminded him of *The Kiss* by Rodin.

A slightly transposed Immaculate Conception metaphor
That also moved a chain of mountain in the process.

A Greek statue was instead early Roman.

He was reminded of how 'non-quaint' the city of his dreams was.
Finally, his virulent anti-monarchal leaning
made for careless nomenclature.

And so it came about that, in his heart of hearts,
Some of his poetic imagery was teetering on collapse
At the rate of the red ball pen ink strikes from the critic.

He then noticed large circles and outlandish squiggles on the page
Acting as magnifiers around an errant dangling preposition:

When Hemingway's words came to his mind… .

Esthetics of Cruelty

Offensive art versus offensive military weapons

Unimaginable degradation of flesh and morality.
Disrespect of societal values and bourgeois sensitivities.
Purposeful visual imposition of carnal hedonism and gratuity.

Assault on all and any commandments.
Insults of all canons and symbols.

Ingenious search for previously off-limit sanctity:
Nuns' habits turned into fertile background for unbridled sexuality.

The viewer, now back on the romantic Parisian streets,
Feeling pings of sinful thoughts
Among echoes anchored in childhood catechism,

Produced by the reptilian sensations of uncontrollable sensual excitement
From the still swirling images of intertwined flesh in various states of ecstasy…

Finding moral solace in the non-lethal conclusion
In the peace of an orgasmic induced sleep,

Purifying the real obscenity of the bloodletting
From the legions of the religious righteous.

Inspired by the concurrent events of the Musée d'Orsay exposition on the Marquis de Sade Attaquer le soleil *and the real evil of the Charlie Hebdo killings in Paris…*

Raw Talent

To the sound of "Eminence Front" by The Who

Raunchy, unapologetically self-absorbed drum beat:
A world of its own.

Heart-skipping drum-skin hits: like some arrhythmia.

Quasi-crystalline pearls from the right side of keyboard:
Giving a surprising lyricism
To testosterone environment.

Late deep-bass guitar entry:
Akin to visions of childhood chills of big bad wolf
And what, according to parental admonishment,
Is the sort of danger he represented for the soul.

Then musical space opens up to the human side:
To vocals, with hints of plaintive angst.

And throughout… this splendid spontaneity
Of early-cut garage-recording freshness of less than polish sheen.

Making the listening feel like voyeurism:
Like a furtive glance at the source of the sound.

It is pure raw talent playing with possibilities.
Not unlike a budding painter:
Building the infrastructure on the blank canvas

Or a poet… and his coalescing imagery:
Instinctively knowing where it will lead,

Both artists without much more than charcoal sketches
And still awkward phraseology.

The creative experience somehow
not wanting to end its own process.

In a cross-fertilizing fashion the band:
Reacting to each other's notes as they escape the studio.

Iconic artistic effort, so well known to the creative act,
That of laying down a piece in the intimate now
and idealizing it into the *later.*

Free Lunch

Prompted by the author's visit to an exhibit of incredibly talented but unrecognized local artists.

The proverbial fifth wheel.
The loving but unloved child.

The iconic starving artist in his Parisian fifth-floor.

Exquisite dexterity of brushstroke
Hints within hints of undercoats of hues

Giving the stone wall on a hill
The aura of a religious artifact.

The painting seems to be a self-contained universe
Of balanced perfection,

Where any addition or subtraction
From a wayward contact with the canvas,

Would have had the effect of producing a still-birth of a world
Instead of this gem,
Hanging lonely and badly lit in its corner:

Confirming, nevertheless, the presence of the unrecognized artist
On our side of the splendor of this canvas.

Anecdote from family friend who studied with Pablo Picasso recalling an event in a restaurant when the already very famous artist paid the waiter with a quick sketch on the paper tablecloth.

This as iconic statement of the critical-mass effect of fame after which the relative quality and need of the art and artist are disconnected.

In a More Perfect World…

In homage to Arthur "Big Boy" Crudup and Billy Eckstine [et al]

In the plasticized Hollywoodian version,
Moses had become everything to everyone
On both sides of the enigmatic Hebraic pattern
Of a baby's swaddling cloth.

Prophetic good looks
In an otherwise outrageously cinematographic coloring
Of proper muscular progeny
And the easy envy of goddesses on earth.

While, from the enslaved ghetto,
An earthly hurtful knowing glance of silenced maternal accomplishment
Followed him with each of his quasi-pharaohnic deeds

Akin to these two artists in the quiet of their sitting room
Listening to foreign echoes of their voice in others,

Their avant-garde talent
Usurped by the slime of racial prejudice.

Self-serving inflexible codes of written and unwritten laws
Expressing the fears that often underlie the abuses of power and greed.

Descendants of which have continued,
With the privileged of intransigent societies,

To deny their rightful lineage of artistic nobility
To those with a perceived excess of skin pigmentation.

Arthur "Big Boy" Crudup (August 24, 1905 – March 28, 1974) was an American Delta blues singer, songwriter and guitarist. He is best known outside blues circles for writing songs such as "That's All Right," "My Baby Left Me," and "So Glad You're Mine," later covered by Elvis Presley and dozens of other artists.

Mobbed by teenage girls wherever he went, Billy Eckstine at one time rivaled Frank Sinatra's popularity.

Jesus… Aspiring Rabbi and Capable Carpenter

A biblically inspired thought experiment

As constructs
Of the human mind that had created them,

The Greeks
Had a way of bringing the gods back to their earthly foundation.

Immersing
Them in the drudgery of marital jealousy and social mayhem

Floating
In petty whims: With accompanying universal consequences.

Turning
The Olympian Fields into the cacophony of a fraternity row.

Is it thus possible, within our daily dust,
That we fail to recognize the worth and wisdom
Under mere human molecules among us?

So there stood… a Jesus:
A distracted, disinterested, underachieving child of a certain
carpenter and inscrutable mother,

Probably rebelling at the thought of squaring pieces of furniture
With his complicated vaporous claims.

We often have had this classic fertile mix
Of misfits with extraordinary ideas.

Along with societal fears that render us blind
To the very brilliance of these misfits.

Taste of the New World

High school lunchroom circa 1960

The hard realities of a new life in the New World
Would eventually prove no match in the questioning of the inherent values of one's culture..

The ingredients were embarrassingly basic:
But apparently with whiffs of proletariat pauperism.

Obvious recycled wrapping.
Aggressively juicy tomatoes and fresh basil:

In a room full of suspiciously pasty orangy-cheeses
And hospital-grade homogenized bread.

Uncontrollable pungency of olive oil aroma
And earthly-cut of Italian bread presentation.

Non-understandable jargon among smirks of disgust:

Rushing to finish this piece of strong evidence:
Of an old world of things and ways.

It is the unspoken truth required by the enthusiasm of her question
That stings the most:

The momentary sacrilegious thought
Toward this woman… and my past

Imposing the role of Madeleines to some of my meals…
To this day.

Immigrant in his first year in the United States un-wrapping his "Mediterranean" lunch, prepared by his mother, to the derision of his American lunch mates.

Exchange Student

Iconic "bise."
Time-wasting ritual at the office upon entrance.
As well as pre-exam small talk and post lunch departure.

A non-sexual and non-gender act
Of simple human solidarity.

Fatherly triple-bise, de rigueur,
For vacationing son on railways platform.

Perfect teaching moment in *La cage aux folles*
When gay father gives fatherly double-bise to prodigal son.

All of this learned, along with algebra homework,
For the betterment of international relations.

American student learns a cultural lesson from a cod-ed classmate from France.

Inspired by kiss on the cheeks given by a woman who has just spent a torrid night with a male character in the original French version of Trois homes et un couffin [Three Men and a Baby]. *American viewers [students] expected a kiss on the lips: hence the different value of the parting-kiss of friendship in the street that would be given to all of her acquaintances, intimate or not.*

The Un-protocoled Internet

The highway thief of the Middle Ages is the computer hacker of today

The temptation… the blindingly palatable Faustian sweetness
Of the gratuitous need met by its subservient offer.

The most demanding intricacies,
The unending alignment of choices,
Reaching at arm's length and then touching the other side of vastness:

Shy antiquities in their finest of high definition,
Monkish manuscripts in their brightest illuminations.

Everything, everyone and every whim seemingly satiated,
With the immediacy of a Gentleman Gentleman's
Anticipated fulfillment by artificial intelligence.

The incestuously close proximity
Of the conceptual and its virtual existence:

Along with a serpentine shape in the Garden
As icons of the most debased imagery, criminal minds and dangers,

Each embedded in the keystroke proximity
Of the latest welcomed family member:
The internet.

Perceiving the highway robber as having been invented along with the empire-changing convenience of such things as the laying of the Roman highway roadbeds.

African Fable

Inspired by J.M.G. Le Clézio "Désert"

In the recycling of life and living,
Is it too much to believe that regeneration,
Of what remains good in us,
Would find a renewed start?

As this fable goes,
A young nomadic woman would lie in the high grass,
In an endless savannah, in the shade of glistening tree leaves.

Opening her thighs full of the pain of birthing,
With hints of sunlight touching her crimson flesh,

She gives in one last cry
Pieces of her entrails to the world:

Hoping that the burst of assertive energy from her daughter
And the seeming quiet respect of the fauna
Is a solemn offering of a better world.

Reflection on the pictures of the horrors inflicted on dislocated people in Africa, the continent believed to have played a major role in mankind's evolution.

... and Injustice for the Rest of Them All *

With the specters of Jonathan Swift and Charles Dickens lurking about.

Scenes worthy of the demented world of medieval horrors:
Poisonous vapors of the unwashed masses.

The deranged and the lost, incestuously living,
Among the detritus of enclosed wealth,
Under the neon signs of the latest numeric wealth.

Cheap panoply assortment of human flesh
On cement sidewalk-display of all shades and degradation.

Various extinction of life kindly and democratically accessed,
Through the purity of refined escapist opiates:
Helped by chrome-plated nine millimeters muzzles.

Streets and neighborhoods all but cordoned off,
For the peace and tranquility of those hurrying by
To do Dow Jones' good work.

Images of peace and five bed roomed tranquility
Put an imperceptible smile on the Escalade driver:

Having duty-fully and knowingly paid his taxes
To ensure his safety in the best of all possible worlds.

* *Ironic paraphrasing of "Equal justice under the law."*

Reflections on the tragic clash of worlds unfolding on the streets between its culture resulting from generational urban abandonment and the police forces saddled with society's demands to impose hands-on application of the concept of order.

A Fatherly Figure

Cogito ergo sum

Ah! This fatherly figure!
The shape behind the curtain.

Not unlike the days of backyard squabbles,
Needing refereeing for choosing sides and arguing rules of game.

Disorganized band of the disheveled
Running to the kitchen window for parental verdict
and transmitted wisdom:

The tradition of the lazy way out.
Anti self-reliant existentialism to the core:
Let Santa Claus guide us.

Politicians without the belief in their own beliefs:
Preferring instead to go back to times
of voodoo medicine and blood-letting:
Of draining humors from the dying body.

Petrified minds reading into their own Caravaggio-reflections.

Reading instead, political messages in the shape of clouds,
Obeying the winds of the cosmos:
Defining what we must choose and do as well as the
variable destinies we face.

Personal responsibilities wrapped in cloth
Of pretty hues and lyrical phraseology.

Giant step backward to pre-Enlightenment
into primordial conscience, nullifying Descartes.

---

* *Reflections on added portion of the Pledge of Allegiance ["One nation under God."]*

Original, more universal pledge of allegiance: "I pledge allegiance to my Flag and the Republic for which it stands, one nation, indivisible, with liberty and justice for all."

The Accidental American

On the third day of sailing
Her new hellish world had reached a routine.

Her body started to ignore putrid smells…
Of bodily functions…
And shouts of despair.

Understandingly petrified of the worst,
Desperate young girls and angry fathers,
Had cut their ankles to the bone from the chafing

Their right of passage
Paid simply by the pigmentation of their faces.

Their version of the American dream
Would eventually come to the survivors
At the multiple cost of rape, beating and more merciless separations

Between the tears of this woman in shackles
And her progeny enjoying a summer day at a ballpark

An ethically complex equation exists
That has yet to be solved by the rules of conscience and memory.

Reflections on the descendants of a newly enslaved African, chained body to body in the cargo hold of a ship on her way to the new world, and her lineage incongruously enjoying a glorious day of Americana at a baseball game.

IV

GIVING A FACE TO THE ABSURD

Truth in Fiction

Assisted suicide scene from the Science Fiction Film, Soylent Green

Sol: [Thorn is seeing the beautiful images shown in Sol's euthanasia chamber] Can you see it?
Detective Thorn: [choked up] Yes...
Sol: Isn't it beautiful?
Detective Thorn: Oh, yes...
Sol: I told you.
Detective Thorn [humbly] How could I know? How could I... how could I ever imagine...?

Gently and wonderfully introduced
To fairy tales of all sorts and purpose in our youth.

Such as, magical holidays… With evidence of Santa's existence through
the sparkle of his gifts.
Or the last pages of soothing happy endings
in rosy folkloric tales of abandoned children finally
reunited with their parents.

The boogey-man and big-bad-wolf
Conveniently and by all account permanently eradicated
by the forces of good.

As a philosopher had told us:
Things would inevitably get better in the best of possible worlds.

And then we have the undeniable Canons of various beliefs
Of eternal happiness:
If not in this world, at the very least in the next one.

Through art…
We have this imaginative thought-experiment:
An extrapolation into our tomorrows…

A look: At what we have.
And what we are.

Into…
What we could be at the rate and rhythm of our present mistakes.

In a sort of cellular subdivision, ad absurdum of our DNA,
With some infernal copulation with artificial intelligence.

We can envision a multiplication and extension…
Good and bad… into an infinite distance:

The whole thing artistically wrapped in palatable layers of science fiction,

Giving the resulting fermented elixir the reassuring smoothness of fables.

Over a silent cup of coffee,
We realize that the real fiction is,
And has been, from the first instance,

Our religiously-driven desperate attempt to change
That part of the devil that bedevils our nature.

A nature that still retains molecules of the original sin of Darwinism.

We wonder:
What… of our obsession with mundane physical comfort
and primitive sexual appetites?
What… of natural or unnatural reptilian competition
In an all digitized, computer-coded existence?

Who… among us would get or deserve the moral equivalent
Of those willing "furniture*"?

What… of our pivotal Faustian bargain:
That of casting our lot in favor of the benign banality of all
and any future technologies?

Privileges will continue to come with several speeds:
Forcing some us to go at only half the speed to light.
While the precious few will already be toasting their arrival.

And the future Ghettos of tomorrow will have to make do
With outdated, old-fashion thermonuclear heat.

Will it be therefore inconceivable or reprehensible
If… a man we all know… Solomon Roth,[1]
A weird, reflective, acerbic, outsider of a man,

Walked… with his remaining human nobility,
Walked… into the House of Going Home[2] to live instead in splendid blackness?

---

[1] *"Furniture," is this case, an attractive woman who is assigned to the owner of the apartment.*

[2] *Watching the character Solomon Roth "going home" [committing assisted suicide] rather than live with the de-humanizing truth about the food source of the world of Soylent Green: Something to reflect upon faced with the population explosion.*

You Might Not Like What You Find

The pain, the horrible pain… the cosmic pain:

The gloved left hand reaching for the source of resistance deep
in the red sand of Mars.

At the foot of some rounded mound:
A piece of a conceptualized object.

By its right angles and inner perfect circle,
Intricate ridges at regular intervals:

A mind had apparently been there.

The cosmonaut looks up from his kneeling position:
Finds a slightly brighter star in the sky.

The Earth… his home… his kind
And all its pretentious belongings.

Realizing in a very human gulp of sadness,
The fragility… the sweet tender fragility,
The exquisite beauty…

And the unknown endgame value
Of the cosmological equation that equates cognitive conscience
…and Time.

Earthlings finding evidence that other worlds had existed and disappeared and so could ours.

Not unlike the scene of the Planet of the Apes *when George Taylor the captain of the space ship from earth realizes that he has been home all the time and that we can lose it all: "Oh my God. I'm back. I'm home. All the time, it was… We finally really did it."*

Rusty Landscape

Alternate destiny

Powerful granite façades on powerful iconic places:
Grecian inspired frontons as ointments of infinity.

Mankind had laid its indelible markers on the Blue Marble,
With its glorious cities built to glorious past and greater future:

Seemingly immortal metropolises:
These human things… Meant to eternalize humanity.

All these images of concrete illusions,
Infused in the solid accomplishments of fearless Homo Sapiens

Brought along with oxygen bottles for their very mortal lungs,
Playing in the mind of the suited cosmonaut

As he wonders what part of this lifeless landscape through his visor
May be the future reflection of his hometown.

Is the Martian landscape Earth's future?

Giving a Face to the Absurd

To the memory of Greta Green

All the inert solidity of the universe
All this power.

All of these things lurking blindly,
Mindlessly trying to deny our piece of what we are and do:
Life… and living.

The enormous adversary… that represents this unthinking unity
With its cosmic forces.

Uniting in its amoral immemorial cosmic equations
At this moment, in this place
In this space and in this time
Fusing on this bottom left corner of a window frame

In full coordination, unhindered by reflection:
Against a symbolic child.

As we remain committed in our philosophical anger
And our very human tears,

That it is in our very awareness
Of the beauty of that smiling glance

That the fragility of a toddler
Still represents our only continuing hope.

Albert Camus described the absurd as the contradiction, the confrontation of mankind's needs and the unreasonable silence of the world: Looking at a publicly released Face book picture of toddler Greta Green killed by falling bricks while in her grand-mother's arms. [May 2015]

Fall From Perfection

As some of us bons vivants have always leaned,
Life and existence
Seemed to pair themselves fruitfully well
With imperfection, mistakes, missteps
Simple imbalance…

… Just plain dirt and the dirty stuff of life
Not unlike some bloody placental remains.

While deities and their spoke-persons seem to relish perfection
In the privileged chapters of our books of ethics

Herded to live crystalline lives
Eschewing dark corners as the favorite haunts of Lucifer
And thus choose the white of cotton of angels

Life and consciousness seemed to have sprung
From the joy of a little more of chaos

A little less balance
A little more skewed evolution

More imperfection
Spreading unevenly the errant possibilities of
Some concept of direction… any direction.

Not unlike the noise bursting into a blissfully quiet
and undisturbed dull life

Awakened to the disturbing waves of emotions
And change… any change.

To, at the very least,
Create fond memories of the precious individuality of moments.

Reflections on the CERN project between France and Switzerland, which is delving into the origins of the Universe: It seems that the very uneven dispersion of dark matter [hence a deviation from perfection] led to the existence of what we know as space, time and our consciousness of them.

Beasts of Burden

At least it's not a horse

His last pieces of silver
Had passed into the brassière of the youngish waitress.

This to complete the circle of despair:
Bad spring, crying baby and aching back.

Late to his return home and even later to his redemption.

He pushed his suffering mare,
Mother to waiting colt,

Through the slippery stones and briar brush:
Steam pushing out of her lungs,

Dutifully returning him home to his present and future.

And, in the early morning light… to a dead part of the animal kingdom
Over which Mankind had been given such a solemn dominion.

Inebriated Eighteenth Century farmhand leaving a tavern late at night. This image came to mind upon seeing a contemporary version of this inebriated man driving in a cloud of smoky oil and rubber out of rural bar late at night.

My Refrigerator and Me

"The results of your blood test will instantly tell your refrigerator to stock more fruit":
Non-attributed gleeful declaration by a futurist.

The intricacies of the algorithms of the future
Will guide our point of contact
With whatever destinies await us.

Our minds, made of no more than star dust,
will have manufactured the equations:

We need and we shall have our creations create creations.

And not unlike another invention… like the God of Genesis,
We shall sit back and contemplate:
And say and see that it is good.
For it will be flesh of our flesh.

But unlike the matinée cinema-world of grandiose science-fiction leaps,

It will not be in the big things that we will pause and take time to think.
It will not be in mind expanding travels and wormholes to
multidimensional places
That we will have pause to question.

Rather, the sadness will lie more likely in what is infinitely small.

A tinge of Faustian remorse will appear.
In tales of folklore of our distant past.

Quaint and ridiculous things found in time-wasting protocols:
Replenishing our organisms with sustaining energy
In endless holiday meals around overcrowded tables
and road-tired guests.

Bizarre ceremonies of the past
Akin to the ritual of high priests and vestal virgins
Hoping for favors from hidden divinities.

We will be saddened once more

When only their silence will answer us from their soul of blinking lights.

For now machinery, of spectacular abilities,
Will decide on perceived needs.

It is then that we will have a passing nostalgic nod
To a ceremonial under grandmother's chandelier:

Ceremonial used to sustain life
And apparently more than that.

Being the nature of mankind to invent and inevitably use its inventions, machine-entities will come to exist that will control us in a Faustian Bargain made of computer codes.

Don't Worry: They're in Charge

Turning the keys over to neural networks

The bogeyman. The Big Bad Wolf.
Frightening things under the relative blanketed safety of our bed of youth.

One morning, we will find that these night-monsters
Have followed us into our awaken-hours:

Forcing us to sit with them at the breakfast table,
Having been told that they would henceforth be our obedient
co-partners.

We will of course have invited them into our lives;
And have to learn to live in a modern-day Brave-New-World,

Of the miscegenation
Of our willing pulsating flesh with the cold virility
of lines of binary codes.

There will probably be some recalcitrants and contrarians.
Out-dated lyricists of the human heart.

Followers of the Trilogy of…
Happenstance,
The innate surprise of surprises.
And the gentle mist of foggy logic.

All of these found in the quaint concept of chance meetings.

Such things as…
The complete randomness of unforeseen and unforeseeable accidents:
Like sitting across a lunch room table
And looking into the features of the face
Of an unpredictable and gratuitously unpredicted future.

Instead, an ultimate Faustian Bargain,

Will have been written and signed.

Our obsolescent human organs
Will have been made part of an alien New Testament:

Having projected our thoughts and needs unto the universe
And engendered a product…

Incapable of putting us above Itself.

Thought-experiment poem: "Highly reliable predictions": Sample of the phraseology in the speculation of the future in the world of artificial intelligence. So, why not put computers with all present and future technical resources at their disposal in charge; then metaphorically close the door of the laboratory and let the "machinery" take over and see what happens to mankind.

In the Tramway Tunnel

Homage to Eugene Thacker

Furtive glance to the left,
Avoiding the panicked glance of a young mother:
Her baby
Struggling to extract nourishment from a deflated breast.

Toddlers blessedly asleep,
Oblivious to the rumbling of explosions.

In this, an eclectic gathering of unknown neighbors
Readying themselves for eternal friendship.

Nothing said… For nothing to be said
That would divert the laws of blind physics;
Adding to the blind happenstance of this gathering
In the calculus of meaninglessness.

But… for a glorious…. humanly noble act.
Of a measure of what it is… To know,

To know… With prescient pride,
The antithetical value against blackness, of recalling some local folklore:

The one about "Dominique from the second floor"
Who had profoundly slept through the last raid

And the ensuing nervous laughter
Permanently etching the moment into the cement walls.

A microcosm of the nihilistic nature of our existence: A tramway tunnel used as a bomb shelter during World War II for the neighborhood families. It contained the main ingredients of the arbitrary and splendid collective solidarity of the human spirit face to face with universal void.

The Glance Upon the Other

Apology for Albert Camus' "L'étranger"

Unbeknownst to us, our youth contained
The power, the magic of ego-effacement.

These emotional stem-cells that allowed
For our natural malleability in non-judgmental acceptance.

The way a baby accepts maternal beauty:
No matter how objectively unreal.

Akin to the amazement of our immature gaze
In the early landscapes, even if arid, of our youth.

That childlike ability of circular observation.
Of the imagery satisfying our need for the imaginary.

These precious stem-cells,
Part of our early vestment before leaving the gates of Paradise,
When nudity was simply part of being.

An ability to marvel at the black sheen between marbly white thighs:
And not the sin behind them.

The attraction of something physically luscious,
Without the adult prize to pay for its meaning:
Not unlike the Little Prince's pain for loving this particular fox.

A candy store made for and by children.
Stem-cells that disappear at the rate of our growing up.

And thus,
There lies the real injustice… the true abject insults to human consciousness;

The ones hurled at all of us,
From the voids of the absurd:

Nihilism offers no ethical anchoring for the pettiness
Of human slights or bigotry;
And gives equal weight to the pathetic on the human-scale.

Thus, the continuing cosmic injustice of:

"Today… mother died. Or was it yesterday?"
As well as… the meaningless heat-induced murder
Of this heretofore anonymous "Arab."

A personal reflection on Kamel Daoud's presentation on his book Meursault contre-enquête [The Meursault Investigation] *a post-colonial look at Albert Camus' book* L'étranger *where Daoud builds what he regrets is the missing persona of this anonymous Arab.*

Based on the author's non-judgmental and captivated look, as a little boy on a North African scene, of a man on his donkey and his family following on foot behind.[see Index/Notes].

Only One Second

One wonders how the last Dodo bird tasted that night
On the open fire of the beach
Did it contain any prophetic sourness of impinging doom?
Would anyone have cared?

Was there not other food replacement for blissful ignorance
of troubling signs?

And so...
Just as there were other fowls to take up the slack
There remain enough seconds in the following centuries
to appease the soul.

But leave it to poets and those soft souls,
The canaries in the coal mines,
To sing a nervous falsetto of unease
To describe in shades of dark lyricism a stationary world:

Burnt on one side
And frigidly still on the other.

Generally ignored announcement that one second will be lost in 2015 due to the slowing in the Earth's rotation.

Self-Awareness

A quick extension of the left claw.
A sharp bite from venomous fangs.
A swift pull on shreds of clueless flesh.

A swallow of fragments of the universe
To feed its members

This universe that knew how to continue its life
By continuing it with Darwinian logical blindness

With the undisturbed ethics in an ocean of amorality
Which could have instead made these moment the apogee

Until one of its representatives
With no particular physical prowess
And no particular aim

More top heavy and erect then most
Looked back… And had thoughts…

Had a thought…

Upon…This crying child and its vague personal meaning

Majestic genesis of reading safety in the eyes around a night fire
And somehow the coagulation of the first elements
Of the complexity… of being.

Reflections on l'Origine du monde *by Courbet and the visually visceral relationship of our humankind and its splendor in spite of its earthy, steamy and sanguine beginnings.*

The Angle of the Sun… the Song of the Cicadas

Memory is what makes us human

Found in apparent detritus of forgotten flakes of life
[Like so many skin cells on the matrix of living]

A box… On the third shelf of an existence near its end.
Aromatic wood and airtight as pathetic attempts to protect its content
through its flight in time and space.

Faded silver broche. Crinkly laminated Freshman ID card,
Jagged angular greenish concert stub. Broken keychain.
Pictures upon fading pictures of beginnings and ends.

Of embarrassing proms and a last picture of a father
planting summer basil.

The whole, fused in the mind, by the heat of passion:
Images of soothing voices, black and white … multicolored entrances
Into the fertile soil of various rites of passage.

That dance floor still bearing the warmth, akin to a Big Bang,
of the transmutation of its genesis in carnal happiness.

All these and other images and sensations
As his lungs give back to the world of Things… Remnants of Things:

The angle of the sun, the cicadas,
The aromatic oils from the pine groves.
That glance of anticipation, across a Parisian café, into an endless future.

The universe will not have changed its course,
But in this magically delusional instant of continuation,
It will have met its greatest opponent and…

Its greatest creation… human memory.

Last visions… in last moments: Inspired by The Book Thief. *And homage to the* Thinking Reed *by Blaise Pascal.*

The Tree, the Atheist and Nothingness

Homage to Jean-Paul Sartre "La nausée"

Does the spring morning sap know that it is doing the gods' work?
Does its syrupy climb to the still brittle top branches
Feel the shy warmth of the sun?

Does each additional ring in its bark know its circular markings to be just
a Pyrrhic triumph?

———————————————

With the heat of a café crème keeping me well grounded in things,
I take full measure of my humanly arrogant,
Culpability-filled… Responsibility,

Aided by the solidity of my cooperating tree-partner.

It has somehow fallen to both of us, to bear witness
to a youngster's short life
And to try to retard its erasure,

Through our silent presences in this otherwise disinterested landscape.

Looking at a splendid, fifty foot, forty years old spruce tree planted to the memory of a little boy: Not easy to accept how simple photosynthesis can seemingly appear more reverent as a source of veneration of human life.

Vaporous Truths

Homage to Karl Marx

Unappealing metaphor with bad dénouement
Worthy of the sternness of high brow mythologies.

Akin to clueless tramps wandering in absurdist plays:
Those inhabited by temporary characters
Showing hints of delusions of counterfeit eternal happiness.

While the concrete truth will remain out of reach
On the other side of a glass sheen of imprisonment

The greatest tragedy mercilessly befalling
These few that know...
The conscious few,

To them is assigned
The specter of living with the pain... The painful unblinking knowledge,

While others fly in opiate vapors.

Sitting in the international terminal at JFK airport in which apparently generations of birds have been living: thus some conceivably not aware of the reality outside while flying within the panes of glass.

Just a Man in a Turtle Neck

In respectful homage to Carl Sagan

A mundane appearance:
No special effects à la Cecil B. De Mille.
Shouldn't there be some aura?

Maybe transforming vin de table into château wine.
Making some meager vegetable soup feed hundreds.

Bringing life back into a dead toddler dying in her grandmother's arms
from errant falling bricks obeying the laws of gravity.

How do we determine the worth of greatness among us?
What hints would make this shepherd look more wise?
Or this physically diminutive person more relevant? Important?

We will have Carl Sagan's words to haunt us
When we breathe our last gasps of clean air.
Drink the muddy infected water of a stream.

Or die on a dying planet:
Crackling under predicted scorching heat.

He did not give us an easy out:
We could not simply write a check.

He never solved for us the equation
For our continued presence on the planet.

Did not prefer the balm of spirits. Revivals.
Or chest pounding and soothing candle lighting.

Instead he offered stern lessons and professorial tones.
And at the very end, the unattractive prophetic gaunt-look
of recessed eye balls.

Troublesome look of our impending doom reflecting in his very gaze:

And not unlike the gravitational pull of a black hole
His words gave him the splendid and illogical imagery
of *some sort of reverse Big Bang*.

So that starting from an incalculably big universe within other
incalculably big universes

Everything seemed to return to this beautiful entity within a single
mind… his.

Like a cosmic Mister Rogers,
He so gently taught us to be at ease
With the spectacular displays of everything
That had been or ever will be.

All this,
Starting with his own molecules made of the same star dust.

Would we, ourselves, really be wise enough to value a-Jesus-like figure or any other wise person if the message appeared to us under the image of our neighbor down the street?

Author's reaction to Carl Sagan's quasi-testamentary wisdom in the Charlie Gross interview.

The Genesis Revisited: a Fable

In homage to Stephen Hawking

The volcanoes had quieted.
The gigantic reptiles properly killed by massive changes.
Evaporation and precipitation had found a moderate medium.

And not unlike the iconic Space Odyssey scene:
the smartest monkeys did inherit the earth.

The machinery was put in motion
for nature to foster procreation and for mankind to prosper:
and the divinities were happy with their effort.

The kindest way to describe the status upon God's return
is that of a rumpus-room of a dysfunctional kindergarten.

Upon the absence of the teacher:
Paint colors had been used to determine leaders;
the mothers' lunches confiscated by the bigger boys;
window views on the tree-lined courtyard assigned to the privileged.

The commoners' toilets in a state of disgrace,
and vital hygienic paper dutifully taxed.

The roof repairs having been ignored,
plans had been proposed to go study outside.

All was indeed the best in the best of worlds.

Fables end best that end with some ex machina help:
Such as,
a powerful and wise lord.
A beautiful motherly fairy.
A repentant bully.
Any death of the kingdom's evil icon..

And so the time came to assign blame in true fable-fashion.
When a mirror dropped from the ceiling.

A Voltairian view of a deist world revisited by its god who had last seen the earth completed and ready for its destiny: a moderate weather system, plenty of water and air. By all account a good start.

Reflection on Stephen Hawking's speculation that mankind would have a thousand years of survival on earth.

Unmentionables

No… not lacy undergarments!
But more mundane. Pedestrian. Practical.
Repetitive. Bothersome. Technical.
Messy. Sticky. Stinky.
Personal and intimate.

Explosion of population and its bodily needs.
The land overwhelmed and overrun by protoplasm:
Very simply, too many human forms.

The world is beyond euphemisms:
Dignity of life.
Higher philosophical ideals.
Freedoms of all sorts.

Having defined our status as sentient entities
As worthy of a dispensation for our extravagances:
Our abuses of land and animals.

On our way to live in a cesspool of our making:
The acrid smells and weather torments of a dying planet
Will enter our daily lives.

As the necessary use of high-tech equipment to filter our environment
Plays the role of the privileges in old-time aristocracy.

Thus bringing us back full circle
To the fortifications of medieval life to protect the living.

Reflections on a newspaper article about the critical need for modern public hygiene accessories and facilities in overcrowded areas of the world where the population come in regular contact with animal and especially human excretions.

Habitable Zone

Reflection on Kepler-452b in the Cygnus constellation and the statistical possibility of mankind coming into contact with another sentient life.

Deep in the deepest of our future,
Those awful teenage doomsday movies will have entered our reality.

Deep in the deepest of space,
We may meet our neighbors.

Our prophets… will have been clueless speculators and filmmakers.

They will have spoken of this moment to matinees crowds,
among nauseating popcorn smells.

We will have seen this film before…

In throw-away lines, from screaming mayhem:
Provoked by various formed and deformed nightmarish masks
Of this ultimate *Other*.

The process followed by appropriately pompous declarations,
from various marionettes of governments:
Activated for our survival:

Assorted leaders standing in the wings,
In full militaristic fashion for "humanity's way of life".

Religious teachers of all colors: still and always self-assured
of our righteous ways.

Taxi drivers, in expletive-filled diatribes,
Succinctly capturing the scenery of careening traffic.

Teen-agers engrossed in teenage embraces,
Looking up tangentially at these interloping "strangers".

And then the dreamers:
The speakers of vaporous philosophy and the inenarrable…

Taking in, with a human sigh, the exquisitely beautiful…
and yet…

Richly simple cosmological miracle:
Of the consciousness of self… and its extension.

Hoping… but with wise trepidation,
That these entities have the sentient instincts to respect us,

In the same matter that proved our kinship
Within the affectionate motherly glance of a female gorilla
toward her child.

Recognizing the common universality of love in the tenderness of a female gorilla as a marker for a definition of what we would hope a higher civilization than ours would interpret as proof of a spark of the consciousness of living in our own eyes.

GLOSSARY

Absurdism: The general philosophical position that there is a disharmony between life [the awareness of life] and death [or its awareness]. Also, the general belief that therefore there is no divine direction to our existence, [See Albert Camus, Jean-Paul Sartre among others]

"Amédée, or How to get rid of it": [See Eugène Ionesco.]

Artificial Intelligence [know as AI]: The author's favorite target for attack and scrutiny. It is the ultimate Faustian Bargain, which humanity cannot, unfortunately, avoid. The hellish world of our refrigerator that would play the role of a housemate is bothersome.

Balzac [see Honoré de]: Prolific French writer. In this book it is his interest, in a short story, in a woman's sensual and sexual complexity.

Baudelaire, Charles: particular reference in this text to the poet's struggle with his corrupt tastes and echoes of innocence. [in particular his *Les fleurs du mal.*]

Billie Holiday: Beautifully talented black singer whose general life and background give a hauntingly dramatic legacy,

Bise [of Kiss in French]: Particularly French ritual of kissing. It is required with certain friend [a hand shake would be an insult]. It is essentially genderless and not intimate or sexual: hence fathers have traditionally and regularly kissed their sons.

Bridges on the Seine: Much imagery in this book is from the numerous vistas from the Seine. The reference to the "locks" is the presence of the latters on one of them put there by lovers. In particular, the very romantic' Pont des artistes.

Caravaggio: Italian artist at the turn of the 17th century was known for his ability to realistically capture moments of human emotion, often in violent depictions of Christianity's sacred stories. Caravaggio's tortuous personal life and demons put him in the brotherhood of Baudelaire and Villon.

Cosmic symmetry: [see "Fall from Perfection"] interesting concept of cosmology that a more perfect dispersion of matter after the Big Bang could have led to no chemical and or physical change to the universe and hence no Earth and its life: Hence intellectual contradictory situation that imperfection is good.

Courbet, Gustave: French painter whose graphically carnal l'Origine du monde [the Origin of the World] is mentioned in the Musée d'Orsay exhibit. [see Sade]

Cyrano de Bergerac: Important character of Edmond Rostand who stand as the epitome of the importance and lasting value of the beauty of the soul over simple physical stature.

Daoud, Kamel: Writer of the post-colonial Franco-Algerian literature. His "Meursault Investigation" ["Meursault contre-enquête"] comments during a presentation of his book, prompted more self-reflection on this personal topic. Very generally, it is in the reference of the social and historic meaning of the use of "l'Arabe" ["the Arab"] in "The Stranger." Kamel Daoud makes a very profound observation that a Frenchman in Algeria calling someone by that name is projecting his own presence on this foreign land. While, Daoud continues noting in his speech that, with all French colonialists out of Algeria, what would the remaining inhabitants call each other? He adds: would a black man in black Africa refer to another man as black? This declaration by the Algerian writer brought me to a moment of my youth in Morocco when I observed what would or should have appeared unusual to an outsider [le regard de l'Autre] the Other's Glance. Instead as a little boy I had the still natural and non-judgmentally gaze of early youth [the blank slate innocence that I call "stem cells" in the poem]. It is latter in life that one learns to categorize people and things as "normally" different: Not unlike these cute animal video scenes of predators raised from infancy with their natural preys in complete accord. The scene referred to in the poem ["The Glance upon the Other"] was that of the father of a family on a donkey, with his wife and children on foot keeping up behind. It was only later that I became aware that there were walls of sociological mores and acculturation to define us from that Other. [see "Evolution and Stasis: Representation(s) of the Maghreb in the Works of Loti, Gide, Camus and Le Clézio." Jean-Yves V. Solinga [University of Connecticut]

Disponibility: from the French word, Disponibilité: As used by André Gide, meaning to make oneself available, opened to nature and experience.

Dora Bruder: Novel by Patrick Modiano about World War II and the Nazi occupation France. [see Occupation]

Édith Piaf: Naturally gifted singer who survived emotional and sexual abuse and managed to channel this anguish into her music,

Eiffel Tower: in this book the vital reference to a nightly spectacular and romantic lightshow of sparkling lights. As well as the "asymptotic' curves of the tower.

Esmeralda: Green-eyed Gypsy woman [hence "emerald"] for whom Bishop Frollo has an uncontrollable lust in Notre Dame de Paris.

Existentialism: a general philosophy of the individual's un-transferable responsibility for his actions through which he defines himself. [see Jean-Paul Sartre]

Fonda, Jane: Chance meeting [a rare autobiographical specificity in my writing]. She plays an integral part [through her iconic image] in the tone of this "Manifesto-right-of-passage." Upon arriving in New York and hours of flight we were still in conversation and I had not realized that we were surrounded by the authorities upon coming out of the plane: hence the question from the Federal Agent: "Are you alone… Miss Fonda?"

Hemingway, Ernest: of interest in this book for his novel *The Garden of Eden* [published posthumously] which offers a more nuanced view of Hemingway's sexuality. We now know that his relationship with his mother [who called him "Ernestine"] along with other revelations could explain the importance of this unfinished novel in understanding the man.

Henry Miller: American writer who penned sexually charged Parisian scenes, which contrasted with the mores of America at that time.

Hirsute: means "hairy or shaggy."

Honoré de Balzac: *La fille aux yeux d'or* [*The Girl with the Golden Eyes*] in which the writer turns his interests to bisexual topics and emotions as well as emotions in love triangles.

Huguenots: French Protestant sect massacred on Saint Barthélemy day in Paris streets.

Île de la Cité [Île saint Louis]: islands in the middle of the Seine in the center of the city. Notre Dame de Paris is on the former.

Inspector Clouseau: the reference in the book is to Peter Sellers, known to have mimicked and adapted for his scenes the particular English pronunciation of his French landlord.

Ionesco, Eugène: French playwright known for its absurdist themes. "Amédée, or How to get rid of it" is a play of the unstoppable and overwhelming presence of the guilt from a prior act that one tries to forget.

Jeanne Moreau: Famous French actress of the last century with that "French pout."

Jeu de Paume [le musée du]: newly restored and modernized museum at the far-end of the Jardin des Tuileries. The building was the site of Serment du Jeu de Paume where critical republican ideals and ideas were publicly discussed and adopted at the end of the eighteenth century.

Jim Crow: poems like "A Place at the Table" is the author's continuing reaction to his relative full acceptance as a white immigrant in American society while multi-generational descendants of black slaves were still carrying their innate difference in the streets: As brutally brought up in "Trailways Idyll." An extension of this racial prejudice is examined in the poem "In a more perfect world" as it pertains to the musical arena. Arthur "Big Boy" Crudup and many others wrote songs that white singers like Elvis would later make famous.

Kasbah Udayas: Impressive Kasbah at the entrance of the city of Rabat in Morocco.

Last Tango in Paris: Film about sexual descent into self-destruction with Paris as a backdrop.

Le Clézio, Jean-Marie: French writer who has lyrically written about the Other, the desert and the Maghreb [North Africa].

Mai Van On: Vietnamese who rescued an injured American bomber-jet pilot from drowning during the war. That pilot was John McCain.

Malle, Louis: Director of the autobiographic "Au revoir les enfants" where reigns an unblinking bitter sweetness about his short friendship with a doomed Jewish student in whom he had met his intellectual match.

Marché saint Denis: Famous street Market on the street of the same name.

Maya Lin: Artist who designed the Viet Nam War Memorial wall which in the author's opinion is an extraordinary statement of tactile witnessing to the more than sixty thousand causalities. A second memorial was erected considered less ambiguous by the presence of military figures on patrol.

Metamorphosis of Ovid: By Auguste Rodin, is the sculptor's study of sexual identity or duality.

Modiano, Patrick: novelist of the Nazi Occupation of France

Monet, Claude: considered the father of Impressionism.

Movable Feast: [see Hemingway and Androgyny]

Musée de Mormottan: precious smaller museum where resides the Monet painting, "Impression soleil levant" through which was coined the whole movement.

Musée d'Orsay: Exhibit on the "moral" violence associated with the Marquis de Sade. It included many of the works of artists who used their art to challenge mores but as the poem "Art and Reality" states no one was physically hurt as compared to the real moral outrage taking place at the same time down the street at Charlie Hebdo apparently, among other things, in the name of some religious concept. [see "Esthetics of Cruelty"]

Musset, Alfred de: In this text, in reference to his poem "Rolla" about the anguish and guilt of a debauched man and the sight of a young prostitute.

Neural networks: [see Artificial Intelligence] A slightly dry euphemism for the smartest of the latest programs, machines and concepts that will reach the critical mass of cogeneration of biology and machines that one of the poem describes as the ultimate Faustian bargain.

Noilly Prat: Herbs-infused apéritif wine.

Occupation: more specifically Nazi occupation of France after its military fall. It imposed a coexistence and practical cooperation which can be jadedly dismissed as weakness by those who have not lived it. The occupation, as one might guess, was made up and related to me as an untidy mixture of resistance by some and collaboration by others. One poem refers to a lesser known memorial to the Shoah and more specifically to the deportation of Jews from France. It is on the island of l'île de la Cité, next to Notre Dame de Paris.

Oued: Moroccan word for river. Oued Sabou goes through the city of Kenitra [the former Port Lyautey] where the Americans landed at the beginning of the North African campaign of WWII.

Pascal, Blaise: whose "thinking reed argument" is one to the great statement about mankind's ability to reflect upon itself and purpose. [see also René Descartes' cogito ergo sum]

Place Pigalle: One of Paris night life center.[see Sacré Coeur]

Primo Levi: Italian writer known for his writings about the Shoah.

Renoir, Pierre-Auguste: French artist who was a leading painter in the development of the Impressionist style. A celebrator of beauty, and especially feminine sensuality to practically the hour of his death.

"Return from Paris" [Notes]:
—Place Blanche: Neon-lit square of the night life of Paris.
—Iconic quote of the 70's French movies-scene: "Je t'aime moi non plus." Nihilistic view of love and love-making. It means "I love you. Neither do I."
—The American writer and actor respectively, Henry Miller and Marlon

Brando made sex and Paris synonymous in their "Tropic of Cancer" and "Last Tango in Paris."
—Jim Morison of the Doors is buried at the Pierre Lachaise cemetery.
—Noilly Pratt is a sweet alcoholic herbal aperitif.
—Yes, it is Jane Fonda next to me on the plane going back to New York [in tourist class].
—Mai Von On, according to public documents ignored the anger of the North Vietnamese around him and pulled a drowning American bomber-jet pilot who turned out to be the future Senator McCain. The reference to President Nixon's prolonging the war is mentioned because I was drafted months after the future president had said, when running for office, that he had "a plan for peace," which from post-publications turns out to be a less than truthful fact.

Rimbaud, Arthur: Famous and incredibly gifted poet. He was romantically linked to Verlaine. The latter, in a fit of jealousy, shot and wounded Rimbaud who practically disappeared from France and by all account never wrote poetry again.

Rodin, August: French sculptor best known for "The Kiss." The poem "Androgyny" inspired by his sculpture "The Metamorphosis" which depict details of sexual ambivalence.

Sacré Coeur: White limestone church at the top of Montmartre in Paris. [In this book, contrasted to the night life at the bottom of the hill at the Moulin Rouge]

(de) Sade, Marquis: ground breaking writer and philosopher whose reputation as a libertine overshadowed his avant-garde notions of advocacy for unrestricted freedom from religion, morality and the law in the arts and for the artist.

Salvador Dali: Surrealist artist famous for his melted clocks and iconic battle with time.

Semprùn, Jorge: French-Spanish writer about the Shoah whose powerful imagery continues to affect my poetry.

Senghor, Léopold: Reading Senghor for the first time during my university years was a literary, esthetic and philosophical revelation. His "À New

York" had the same elements of the outsider involving Africa, France, America, Francophony, Anglophony bathed in the music of a poet. I can't walk the Seine and the bridges at night without his presence in the reflection of the city lights in the water.

Spektor, Regina: referred to in this book for the touching lyricism of her song "Samson" to which I was pleasantly introduced by accident, since I unfortunately had not known of the song or the singer until then.

[le] Train bleu: [the Blue Train] Name of earlier French high speed train made famous for its travel between Paris Gare de Lyon and the Côte d'Azur [hence the name and the color of the cars]. It left from this iconic station home of the Orient Express. The upstairs of the station has always had a chic restaurant with, to this day, a marvelously historic ambiance.

"[In the] Tramway Tunnel": deals with a slightly fictionalized real life event that took place ironically during a bombing raid by the Allies over the city of Marseille, France.

Vadim, Roger: French movie director who used Jane Fonda [his future wife] in a bizarre science-fiction sex odyssey. ["Barberella"]

Verlaine, Paul: Poet of the romantic movement. Romantically linked to Arthur Rimbaud. [see Rimbaud]

Viet Nam War: [see Manifesto, Maya Lin] [see Manifesto, Jane Fonda]

Villon, François: Medieval poet haunted by the duality of the unapproachable muse [the Madonna] and his dissolute personal life.

Woodsworth, William: of "The hour of splendor in grass" fame, for the particular reference in this book.

World War I: Event that had an existentialist effect on parts of the European societies: It introduced horrors of an avoidable, insanely parochial war to arguably the more civilized example of mankind's evolution. This book takes the occasion of the centenary of the conflict for some reflection as one peripherally touched by the survivors of the war: in this book, for instance, a boyhood friend's father whose introduction to me was akin to seeing a ghost [the old soldier had been a victim of gas warfare].
[see addendum note to "Sleepwalkers of World War I"]

Index

Titles in bold and first lines in italics.

Aberration of the soiling of intimacy,	*73*
Accidental American, The	**94**
Acculturation: Sounds of Snapping Crust.	**79**
African Fable	**91**
Ah! This fatherly figure!	*93*
All the inert solidity of the universe	*101*
All will be fine now in the great temple of illusions:	*50*
ambiance was artificially cooled: The	*66*
…and injustice for the rest of them all	**92**
Androgyny	**70**
Angle of the Sun, The… The Song of the Cicadas	**113**
Appetite and Disdain	**73**
Art and Reality	**74**
As constructs 87	
As some of us bons vivants have always leaned,	*102*
As the lights on the Eiffel Tower start to sparkle	**11**
As though the very gentleness of the colors	*52*
Asymptotes at the Infinity of Passion	**15**
Beast of Burden	**103**
Beautiful Baby, A	**46**
Between the Jehovah Witness and the S&M Prostitute	**63**
Billie Holiday and Édith Piaf	**76**
calluses on his hands, The	*61*
Certain Languor in her Eyes, A	**17**
certain languor in her eyes, A	*17*
Clarity…	*56*
Constructive Criticism	**81**
Convergence	**54**
Cyrano: a fable	**67**

Deep in the deepest of our future,	*121*
Does the spring morning sap know that it is doing the gods' work?	*14*
Don't Worry They're In Charge	**106**
Emotion Recollected in Tranquility	**24**
Erased Moments	**14**
Esthetics of Cruelty	**82**
Exchange Student	**89**
Fall from Perfection	**102**
Family gatherings when past issues are revisited	*51*
Fatherly Figure, A	**93**
Found in apparent detritus of forgotten flakes of life	*113*
Free Lunch	**85**
French Kiss	**79**
From both sides of the canvas	**26**
Frozen Land	**6**
Furtive glance to the left,	*108*
Genesis Revisited, The	**118**
gentleness in his consciousness of life, A	*5*
Gently and wonderfully introduced	*96*
Giving a Face to the Absurd	**101**
Glance upon the Other, The	**109**
Glorifying awe,	*31*
Good flour, yeast, salt, water.	*79*
Grand child for a new century.	*46*
Habitable Zone	**121**
hard realities of a new life in the New World, The	*88*
He did not tower over people:	*67*
He first appeared in the sulfurous fumes of Freedom	*38*
He had always been in awe of this man:	*78*
He was known as the Pyramid:	*55*
higher wall and different color, A	**50**
His last pieces of silver	*103*
Historical Monument 3rd Quarter of Twentieth Century	**56**
Human Face of Destiny, The	**55**
I did not sit down simply to have something to eat or drink.	*68*
Iconic "bise."	*89*

Improbable beauty of the flowers of evil,	*76*
"I'm so sorry... I can't honestly commit to anything."	*57*
In a More Perfect World	**86**
In a world... where the viewer has the nagging feeling	*74*
In Lieu of a Painting	**27**
In Paris: Saxophone solo	**13**
In the plasticized Hollywoodian version,	*86*
In the recycling of life and living,	*91*
In the Tramway Tunnel	**108**
Inner Sanctum	**29**
intricacies of the algorithms of the future, The	*104*
It is later in life	*30*
It is not enough to have means.	*8*
It seemed as though all the objects around her	*23*
It was her...	*45*
It was not the piles of boxes,	*80*
Jesus… Aspiring Rabbi and Capable Carpenter	**87**
Just a different modifier:	*79*
Just a Man in a Turtle Neck	**116**
Last Supper	**21**
Le train bleu	**8**
Let the notes gently glide in beads of softness over her taunt muscles:	*29*
Lifted...	*2*
Luciana	**7**
Madeleines	**80**
Man of ardent fervor ... an artist.	*15*
man with an excellent image, A	*43*
Multi-layered anxiety.	*44*
Multiple Realities	**57**
mundane appearance: A	*116*
Musical phrase coming up…	*13*
My Refrigerator and Me	**104**
No gothic-beauty setting:	*32*
No... not lacy undergarments!	*120*
Nobility of Frailty, The	**31**
Of Gypsies Jews and Others	**59**

On the third day of sailing	*94*
One wonders how the last Dodo bird tasted that night	*111*
Only One Second	**111**
Outside ice and snow:	*6*
pain, the horrible pain... the cosmic pain: The	*99*
Perfume of the Gods, The	**23**
Personal Conscience and Collective Absolution	**53**
Place at the Table, A	**68**
Place of obscene contrast.	*63*
Post Modern Woman, A	**69**
Powerful granite façades on powerful iconic places:	*100*
proverbial fifth wheel, The	*85*
purity... The unfiltered nature of it, The	*9*
Putting a period at the end of the poem	*24*
quick extension of the left claw, A	*112*
Random Morsels	**9**
Raunchy, unapologetically self-absorbed drum beat:	*83*
Raw Talent	**83**
Reciprocal glances between passing souls,	*62*
Reflected Gaze	**30**
replaceable soldier, The	**38**
Rising from the mud	**45**
Robust carefree abandonment of energy.	*60*
Rorschach Inkblot Test	**44**
Rusty Landscape	**100**
saintly father, A	**51**
Sanctuary	**32**
Scenes worthy of the demented world of medieval horrors:	*92*
Seeing... as merely reconstructions:	*75*
Self Awareness	**112**
setting seemed more than appropriate: The	*42*
She had overpowered him,	*70*
She saw their presence on this bed, in this room,	*36*
Shrapnel of Love	**52**
Silky Reality	**75**
Simply wanting to capture the vaporous nature of her hair.	81

Index

Sleepwalkers of World War One	60
Splattering intimacy with searing adjectives:	27
Stomach still grumbling after meager rice and invisible protein meal.	54
Stone Dust	78
Successful Life, A	43
Sunday pastries after church and apéritif at the bistrot de la gare,	49
Surface texture, smelling of life itself.	26
Symbolic translucence of pinkish softness.	7
Taste of the New World	88
temptation... the blindingly palatable Faustian sweetness, The	90
The bogeyman. The Big Bad Wolf	106
Their bodies had opened:	34
There are those who have loved.	14
There was an intriguing ambivalence about her:	69
There was no presence of sharp-edged desert stones,	59
These were not happy times for a seven year old little girl:	48
Through a child's eyes	48
Through a child's eyes II	49
Torture of the energy of images and sounds.	21
Trailways idyll	66
Train Engineer, The	61
Tree the Atheist and Nothingness, The	114
Tremors from the Universe	34
Tremors from the Universe II	36
Truth in Fiction	96
Ultimate Sensations	5
Un-protocoled Internet, The	90
Unappealing metaphor with bad dénouement	115
Unbeknownst to us, our youth contained	109
Une certaine lassitude dans les yeux	19
Une certaine lassitude dans ses yeux:	19
Unimaginable degradation of flesh and morality.	82
Unmentionables	120
Vaporous Truths	115
virility of the musical pulse, The	11
Voice from Company C 4th Platoon, A	42
volcanoes had quieted, The	118

We… We didn't do anything wrong 62
White Absolution 2
Worse and more shameful wars had been and would be fought. 53

You Might Not Like What You Find 99

About the Author

Jean-Yves Solinga

Jean-Yves' family comes from Provence. He was born in Algeria, and lived thereafter between the south of France and Morocco in what he describes as an idyllic youth. Upon settling in America with his family, at the age of 15, he had already been writing poetry: being first published in *A Letter Among Friends* along with John Norman of New London, CT. After serving in the U.S. Army, he began a successful career in teaching and lecturing. Jean-Yves holds a doctorate in French on the representation of the Maghreban [North African] landscape found in the texts by Pierre Loti, André Gide, Albert Camus and Jean-Marie Le Clézio. He has published several books of poetry: *Clair-Obscur of the Soul* (2008), *Clair-obscur de l'âme* [in French] (2008), *In the Shade of a Flower* (2009), *Landscape of Envies* (2010), *Words Made of Silk* (2011), *Impressions of Reality* (2013), and *Artist in a Pixelated World* (2014).

His books offer a singularly unique view of mankind's reflection through the prism of the lyrical language while in the midst of at times impressionistic poetry tackling many hard realities of history and society: Quoting Michael Linnard with "At times, some passages [that] are examples of the translation of the human condition into pure thought."

The author has been a featured speaker at the Alliance Française of New Haven and Hartford; Presented at the Center of the Teaching of French at

About the Author

Yale; The University and Southern Connecticut State University on the use of poetry in language studies; Published in *"Art et poésie"* edited by the renowned French poet Jean-Claude George. He has also read at the Poetry Institute of New Haven; Wesleyan University book store; the Cantab Lounge in Cambridge, the Blue Star Café in Providence, the Guilford Green Barn. He has featured at the Arts café in Mystic; the Hygienics; the Bean and leaf; the Bank Square Bookstore. He has co-featured at the Mystic Art Gallery, and at the Harriet Beecher Stowe Center on the theme of social justice in poetry. Jean-Yves has had poems published by the *Free Poet Collective Ekpharsis Project* at the New Britain museum, the *Ekpharsis Loft Anthology of Providence* and the *Little Red Tree Anthology*, the *Exquisite Project of the Bill Libraries*.

His poetry has been nominated three times for a Pushcart Award. Jean-Yves Solinga is a poet of immense ability and range whose lyricism is truly remarkable. It contains many breathtakingly beautiful and sophisticated poems that reach out to the very limits of the human condition where true art exists. Many facets of his work find inspiration and perspective in his cultural duality. This gives his poems a personal as well as societal breath. In *Asymptotes at the Limit of Passion*, Jean-Yves continues to bring the infrastructure of poetry as close as possible to the realm of the realities of our lives.

www.ingramcontent.com/pod-product-compliance
Lightning Source LLC
Chambersburg PA
CBHW080509110426
42742CB00017B/3053